BRITISH POPULAR BALLADS

British Popular Ballads

EDITED BY

JOHN E. HOUSMAN Ph.D. Dr Iur.

Granger Index Reprint Series

 BOOKS FOR LIBRARIES PRESS
FREEPORT, NEW YORK

First published 1952 as part of the Life, Literature,
and Thought Library by George G. Harrap & Co., Ltd.
Reprinted 1969 by arrangement
Copyright. All rights reserved

STANDARD BOOK NUMBER:
8369-6020-3

LIBRARY OF CONGRESS CATALOG CARD NUMBER:
74-76936

MANUFACTURED
BY
HALLMARK LITHOGRAPHERS, INC.
IN THE U.S.A.

FOREWORD

THIS series aims at presenting in an attractive form English texts which have not only intrinsic merit as literature but which are also valuable as manifestations of the spirit of the age in which they were written. The plan was inspired by the desire to break away from the usual annotated edition of English classics, and to provide a series of books illustrating some of the chief developments in English civilization since the Middle Ages. Each volume will have a substantial introduction, which will relate the author to the main currents of contemporary life and thought, and which will be an important part of the book. Notes, where given, will be brief, stimulating, and designed to encourage the spirit of research in the student. It is believed that these books will be of especial value to students at universities and in the upper forms of schools, and that they will also appeal very much to the general reader.

Grateful acknowledgment is made of the valuable help given to the series in its early stages by Mr S. E. Buckley.

VIVIAN DE SOLA PINTO
General Editor
Life, Literature,
and Thought Library

NOTE

It is deeply regretted that Dr J. E. Housman died on December 6, 1951, and was therefore unable to see this book through the press. I wish to acknowledge the valuable help given to me by Mrs D. M. Housman and Mr G. R. Hibbard in correcting the proofs.

V. DE S. P.

University of Nottingham, 1952

PREFACE

BETWEEN 1882 and 1898 Francis James Child published his great collection of traditional English and Scottish ballads in five folio volumes, in which he offered every known variant of these ballads, prefixing to each a painstaking and scholarly analysis, comparing variants and drawing attention to relevant foreign versions. This collection was primarily for the scholar, and in 1904 Helen C. Sargent and G. L. Kittredge published a one-volume collection for a wider circle of readers, giving one text, at least, of every ballad, and retaining as much of the introductory matter as seemed of general interest. The present volume attempts a further reduction of Child's original work, from which all the texts and much of the introductory matter prefixed to the individual ballads have been chosen.

It is hoped that an edition of this size, uniform with other texts in this series, will stimulate the student to pursue his ballad reading in the larger collections.

The General Introduction in this book is intended to give some account of traditional British balladry from the point of view of recent research, and, without being unduly academic, it endeavours to stress in particular certain social and comparative aspects of the subject.

My thanks are due to my wife, for her untiring help in the completion of this volume, to Professor V. de S. Pinto, for his kind advice on a variety of points, to Mr M. J. C. Hodgart, for his valuable suggestions, and to the Houghton Mifflin Company for their kind permission to quote from Child's original work.

J.E.H.

University of Nottingham, 1951

CONTENTS

INTRODUCTION

ALMOST every student of English poetry numbers among his favourite poems one or two traditional ballads, such as *Sir Patrick Spens*, *Edward*, or *The Wife of Usher's Well*. In these and in many other ballads he moves in an atmosphere poetic beyond a shadow of doubt, yet different from that of any other type of poetry, narrative or lyrical. In his delight in ballads the modern reader knows himself in good company. From Sir Philip Sidney, who "never heard the olde song of *Percy* and *Duglas*" without finding his "heart mooued more then with a Trumpet," the unbroken line of ballad lovers runs via Richard Corbet, a seventeenth-century divine, who at Abingdon Cross helped a ballad-vendor sell his stuff by singing some samples to the crowd, Samuel Pepys, an untiring collector of ballads, Addison, and Goldsmith to the Romantics, with whom the real study and the imitation of traditional balladry began. Rossetti, Morris, and Swinburne show ballad influence at its best during the Victorian era, and modern poets like W. H. Auden and C. Day Lewis have continued to write good narrative poetry inspired by the ballad tradition.

The ballad seems to have come into existence throughout these islands and all over Europe during the late Middle Ages, probably from the late fourteenth century onward. Occasional references to short, popular narrative poems are found before that date, but in the absence of extant texts it is impossible to prove that these poems were ballads in any real sense.

After the introduction of printing in the late fifteenth century a new kind of popular ballad came into existence. This is the so-called 'broadside,' or 'stall' ballad, printed on one side of a sheet of paper and hawked in the streets or sold from stalls at the big fairs. Autolycus, in Shakespeare's *The Winter's Tale*, is the typical seventeenth-century pedlar, who carries among his

other wares a sheaf of ballads, and singles out for praise a
"ballad of a fish, that appeared upon the coast, on Wednesday
the four-score of April, forty thousand fathom above water."
These broadsides were the poetry of the urban proletariat, as
traditional ballads were of the village community. Broadsides
were influenced in form and diction by traditional ballads,
which in turn were influenced by broadsides. In this study
discussion will be concentrated on the traditional ballad as distinct from the broadside.

The traditional British ballad of the late Middle Ages
developed from two main sources—dance songs and narrative
poems. The dance songs (Low Latin, *ballare*—to dance) and
carols[1] of early medieval France gave the traditional ballad its
lyrical characteristics, such as the form of its stanza, its natural
imagery, its refrain, and, above all, its close connexion with
musical accompaniment. A study of these early dance songs
and carols shows a close relationship with the ballad. We
know, also, that the Danish ballad, not dissimilar from English
and Scottish ballads in stanza-form, natural imagery, and
refrain, originated under the influence of the French carol. In
medieval Denmark a singer, accompanied by a fiddler, would
recite a ballad, and the dancers in a ring round them would sing
the refrain in time with their dancing. While some of the form
and imagery of these earlier dance poems was preserved in later
lyrical poetry, developments in poetic and musical technique
tended to separate lyrical poetry and music, from the latter half
of the seventeenth century onward. The simpler traditional
ballad, however, enjoyed by a less sophisticated public than the
lyric, could retain its tune; and ballad text and ballad tune continued as a unit well into the nineteenth century. The relatively
simple forms of the ballad stanza and the frequent occurrence
of refrains helped to preserve this unity. The subject of ballad
music falls outside the frame of this discussion, but it may be
well to mention that ballad text and ballad tune should be
studied together, and that ballad tunes preserved until

[1] 'Carol' here means a song, usually with a refrain, accompanying a round
dance. Originally the word had no religious associations.

comparatively recent times a system of harmony and scale unfamiliar to the student of orchestral or operatic music, but of great beauty and originality.

If medieval French dance songs and carols gave the ballad its lyrical characteristics, much of its earliest subject-matter, and even its general attitude to such problems as war, love, and the supernatural, were derived from older narratives, such as the Germanic epic, the French *chanson de geste*, and the medieval romance. Later ballads continued this tradition, even when their subjects were derived from other sources.

The ballad public was not found in the great courts, but in smaller feudal castles and manor houses, and in the village communities dependent on them. Entertainment was supplied by the travelling minstrel, who moulded the long narratives of epic and romance, suitable only for leisurely circles, into the crisper and more economic form of the ballad narrative. Sung in this fashion, stories were acceptable to the village community; they were easily remembered, and they survived through centuries on the lips of gifted singers. Many of the stories from which these ballads derive were lost. Frequently divergent forms of the ballad remained. When in the eighteenth and nineteenth centuries collectors recorded these ballads from men and women of no literary pretensions, sometimes not even literate, they were faced with a poetic form of uncertain age and authorship, yet clearly with considerable claims of an æsthetic kind. While many ballads did not derive from romances or similar long narratives, but related an event in history, a local feud or love story, they were composed by gifted individuals, working in the tradition of ballad-making and were then transmitted from one singer to another. In this way, such ballads survived on the lips of the people, and, though based on written sources, in course of time they became the property of the people who sang them, moving further and further away from their literary origins. In this sense the traditional ballad is oral literature, and as oral literature it should be sung and heard, not read silently.

II

If we are right in suggesting that ballads were originally composed for the entertainment of the baron and his company, or for the village community so closely linked with feudal society, and that many of our best ballads were collected from the lips of villagers, it seems clear that the ballad supplied musical and verbal entertainment for rural communities, especially valuable in the absence of instrumental music and written literature. In order to fulfil its function as entertainment the ballad had to deal with many possible emotions, and, in fact, its scope varied from the intensely tragic to the broadly humorous, from the sweetly delicate to the starkly terrible. Even if the events narrated were in many cases either timeless or of the past, their setting and the treatment accorded to them were not, on the whole, as unsuitable for the men and women of the village as are the setting and sophisticated treatment of urban literature. We shall find that the overwhelming majority of ballads are set in the country or in the castles of the lesser nobility, while the treatment of the story is fundamentally unreflective, with an absence of that philosophical and speculative generalization dependent on greater leisure than village life permits.

Only comparatively few English and Scottish ballads (as opposed to carols) of a strictly religious character have survived. The miracles of the Virgin, the acts and martyrdom of saints, narrated in innumerable ballads of France, Italy, and other countries of the South, were apparently of no importance in the life of English and Scottish ballad communities even before the Reformation. There remain ballads dealing with New Testament stories, the life of Christ Himself, and we find that the few genuine religious ballads extant are almost exclusively concerned with the life of Christ. It is interesting to note, however, that of the religious ballads in our first section (pp. 61–70) two, *St Stephen and Herod* and *Judas*, are pre-Reformation ballads, and some others may be equally early. In fact no new ballads on religious topics were composed after about 1600. Whether this is due solely to the Reformation and to the lack of a unified religious tradition in this country after the Reformation may be doubted: it serves on the other hand as a startling contrast to conditions in Catholic countries, where the singing of religious ballads on feast-days of the Church has by no means died out. A recent broadcast of the annual celebrations in honour of St Ronan, from Locronan, in the department of Finisterre, where Bretons sang ballads dealing with the life of their local saint, was of interest in this respect.

The comparative absence of religious ballads is counterbalanced, however, by the interest of English and Scottish balladry in the supernatural in all its manifestations. Some of our finest and most gripping ballads belong to this category: from *Tam Lin* to *The Wife of Usher's Well*, from *Thomas Rhymer* to *The Unquiet Grave*, we move in a world where fairy-folk, ghostly creatures of the sea, and the dead, share field and woodland, moor and bracken, house and churchyard with men and women of the workaday world. Nor can fairy-lore be explained away as the imagination of the Celt. Our ballads share this preoccupation with the ballads of Scandinavia. Perhaps the landscape of the North, the lonely moorlands, the rocky foreshores, and the pathless forests were peopled by popular imagination with the elves, mermaids, and other ghostly folk who seem their natural denizens. In these English and Scottish ballads, then, men and women of village and castle and supernatural beings, the quick and the dead, communicate, pay each other visits, intermarry, and pass from one realm into the other. Janet, the heroine of *Tam Lin*, meets the fairy rout in her father's forest, the sons of *The Wife of Usher's Well*, when returning from the dead, behave much as they did in their earthly days.

English and Scottish balladry is also particularly rich in tragic ballads, in the sense that, as in Scandinavian ballads, the terrible effects of passion and unbalanced emotion are faced without too frequent sentimental evasion. The result is sometimes a starkness which invites comparison with the greatest narrative poetry. Tragic emotion in all its variety is to be found in the great ballad scenes; Mary Hamilton on the way to execution, Lord Barnard approaching the guilty lovers, Sir Patrick Spens laughing in the face of an impossible task, the Wife of Usher's Well forced to see her sons rise at cockcrow, never to return. At least one ballad, *Edward*, reaches the strength of Greek tragedy; here we witness the fall of a great house in the harrowing dialogue between a mother, forced by a power beyond her control to goad her son to full confession and to the final blinding curse, and a son, driven from evasion after evasion to a revelation as shattering as it is artistically compelling.

It is, perhaps, not surprising that tragic power is frequently found in ballads dealing with one or other aspect of love. Themes of love are commonly found in English and Scottish balladry without being so all-pervasive as in courtly or Elizabethan lyrical poetry. There is, on the other hand, the great body of historical and quasi-historical ballads in which the manifold emotions of love find little place. Yet, even so, the love of man and woman permeates English and especially Scottish balladry. The ballads are full of both tragic and happy love. It may overwhelm the lovers and lead them to their deaths, as in *Earl Brand* or *Clerk Saunders*, it may lead them to transgress the moral code, as in *Little Musgrave and Lady Barnard*, or its risks and hazards may be a prelude to a happy union, as in *The Gay Goshawk*. In any case love is treated simply, with a strong faith in 'true love,' and an open distaste for mercenary motives. Social responsibilities are frequently stressed, as is the tragic conflict of love and duty. Ballads like *Earl Brand* and *Clerk Saunders* derive much of their poignancy from the conflicts arising as a result of the irreconcilable loyalties due to lover and to kin.

Many English and Scottish ballads deal with historical subjects. It is significant that there are only a few genuine traditional ballads, as opposed to broadside ballads, dealing with really important events in history. The traditional ballad does not serve as a popular chronicle. Whether we deal with such magnificently dramatic accounts of border warfare during the late fourteenth century as in *The Hunting of the Cheviot*, with incidents from the great age of the moss-troopers as in *Jock o the Side*, or with sixteenth- and seventeenth-century clan feuds as in *Edom o Gordon* or *The Fire of Frendraught*, the events described are scarcely ever related to outstanding events in national history. They are treated in ballad-form because of local interest, which invested them with importance for the men and women of the district, and the absence of such local interest may help to explain why a number of outstanding events in the history of England and Scotland were not treated in ballad-form. Three outstanding ballads dealing with events of the sixteenth century, and probably composed soon after these events occurred, refer to incidents that it would be difficult to trace in an average school history. *Johnie Armstrong*, a ballad of great tragic power, telling of the seizure and heroic death of a Border robber in the time of Henry VIII, exists in three versions, and was popular soon after the hero's death. The exact historical background of this ballad is known only to experts in the knotty problems of Border history. *Mary Hamilton* exists in over thirty versions, and this fine ballad has set a major puzzle for Scottish historians. The ballad ostensibly relates the execution of a maid-of-honour of Mary, Queen of Scots, for infanticide, but no record exists of a Mary Hamilton having been one of the Queen's personal servants or having met a fate similar to that of the heroine of the ballad. Courthope, on the other hand, drew attention to the striking coincidence between the central incident of the ballad and the execution for infanticide of a Scottish girl by the name of Hamilton at the court of the Russian Emperor, Peter the Great, early in the eighteenth century. Yet the ballad as it stands betrays at no point any but Scottish origin. It is written with a detailed knowledge of Edinburgh, and whoever composed it knew the names of two at least of Mary Stuart's attendant ladies. Finally, *Edom o Gordon* refers to an incident during the Scottish troubles of the 1570's, after Mary Stuart's flight. The event is historically localized in Aberdeenshire, but it is so obscure that it has been impossible to discover whether the ballad gives an accurate account of the occurrence. In the case of many other Scottish ballads, both from the Border and from the more central portions of the Lowlands, the historical nucleus is extremely hard to establish with certainty. Historical accuracy is obviously of secondary importance for the ballad-maker, for whom, as for any poet, character, situation, and conflict—in short, what might or ought to have happened—is infinitely more important than what did happen in sober inartistic fact. For this reason the historical ballad seems at its best when dealing with situations of conflict, just as the ballad of love is at its most effective when a conflict of loyalties between the loved one and the family, between a wife and a mistress, lies at the centre of the plot. In the historical ballad, too, the conflicts inherent in the situation of the Border— between English and Scottish or between the moss-troopers and the authorities, or in Scotland itself between contending parties or rival clans—produce the finest ballad poetry. The pathos of *Bonnie James Campbell*, as puzzling from the purely historical aspect as it is moving poetically, derives from a society in which sudden death and the perils of manhood contend with the love of home and family in an irreconcilable tension. Conflict between an individual, wronged or rebellious, and the forces of Government is one of the most important sources of this type of ballad. On the whole, the ballad is in sympathy with the outlaw, the moss-trooper, the poacher, as long as he does not show wanton cruelty, lack of sympathy with the poor, or licentiousness. There is a sturdy sense of the value of the individual as opposed to the unjust encroachments of Government in these ballads, as there is manifest delight in the courage, cunning, and resourcefulness of the individual or group of individuals at bay. Although ballad-narrative is, on the whole, impersonal, there can be little doubt with whom the poet sympathizes in the ballads of *Johnie Armstrong* or *Jock o the Side*, quite irrespective of the historical rights and wrongs of the case. When the attackers have got the better of Johnie Armstrong and his gallant band Johnie says:

Fight on, my merry men all,
   And see that none of you be taine;
For I will stand by and bleed but awhile,
   And then will I come and fight againe.

On a different and much less exalted level the same ideals permeate ballads of outlaws, such as the long account of *Adam Bell, Clim of the Clough, and William of Cloudesly* (Child, No. 116), and the famous series of ballads associated with the name of Robin Hood. We are not concerned here with discussing in detail the complex historical and mythological data which may have gone into the shaping of these stories. About Adam Bell and his comrades we know little of a historical nature. What concerns us here is the obvious sympathy of the ballad poet for the outlaws, the tender sentiments of family love which the poet depicts in them, and, perhaps most significant, the insistence on the King's impartiality in dealing with the band, which, as in certain of the Robin Hood ballads, amounts to a preference on his part for the manly independence and accomplished skill of the outlaws rather than for the humdrum rectitude and fundamental inhumanity of the forces of law and order. The King, in idealized medieval fashion, judges people according to their moral fibre, and not solely from reasons of self-interest.

The Robin Hood ballads exhibit this triangular relationship to perfection, again with unmistakable sympathy for the outlaws and especially for their leader, and a clear emphasis on the idealized King's preferences. Indeed, the realization of the tension between the accomplishments and humanity of the outlaws and the stupidity and inhumanity of the Sheriff of Nottingham, as the representative of society, is a common feature of the series of Robin Hood ballads composed during widely different periods, and varying considerably in poetic merit. Again, as in the case of *Adam Bell*, it is the spirit of the ballads that counts, the heroic strain of a struggle of men fundamentally good, and beyond doubt accomplished in many skills and crafts, against the dull representatives of a society which has found no place for the energies of the outlaw. Add to that the happy comradeship of woodland life, the high sense of social honour and decency shown by Robin Hood and his men, the brave bearing of Robin Hood, when, like many epic heroes, he dies as the result of treachery, and the connexion with heroic ideals is evident.

It is perhaps not surprising that there are many ballads in which the humorous and satirical elements preponderate. Whether they deal with instances of popular cunning victorious over more cultured intelligence, as in *King John and the Bishop* (Child, No. 45), or with matrimonial troubles, as in *The Wife wrapt in Wether's Skin*, the humour is of the broad, unsophisticated kind. In the best of these ballads we move in the world of Chaucer's realistic tales, and their comedy becomes an expression of faith in the essential wholesomeness of everyday life.

III

In assessing the value of the traditional ballad as poetry, it should be remembered that the ballad is a true and separate form of poetry, not a miniature epic or a lyric with narrative additions. W. P. Ker's fundamental essay "On the History of the Ballads" in *Form and Style in Poetry* makes this point clear, and it is supported by his unrivalled knowledge of British and European balladry. He emphasizes that the ballad poet exercises instinctive judgment as to subjects that can be treated as ballads. The rambling romance of the Middle Ages, the full-fledged epic, the transcript of history (attempted unsuccessfully in the Icelandic *Skotlands Rímur*) are all equally unsuitable because they lack the concentration and the insistence on essentials of the true ballad. Subjects of epic and romance can be treated in ballad-form, but they must undergo a fundamental change. Thus, as W. P. Ker points out, the Icelandic ballad of *Tristram and Iseult* is successful because its author did not merely transcribe the leisurely account of the Norwegian saga of Tristram, but, by combining narrative economy and selection of relevant incident with lyrical grace of a high order, transformed the romantic saga into a true ballad. The same holds true of the Nibelung saga, treated by medieval German poets with all the pomp and circumstance of the epic, but endowed by later Danish ballad poets with a new narrative unity, condensed, shorn of inessentials, and lyrically heightened. In the same way the epic story of Hilde-Kudrun, told in the medieval German minstrel epic *Kudrun*, survives in German, Swiss, Scandinavian, Spanish, and Yugoslav ballads in supremely concentrated form. Only the central incident of a princess forced by an envious mother-in-law or hostile queen to perform menial tasks, and of her brother recognizing her and avenging her shame, is retained. The medieval German epic, on the other hand, tells the full, complicated history of the girl's wooers, and sets the story into a detailed background of chivalrous exploits, with very archaic overtones of heroic Germanic story. In the most beautiful ballad version, the Spanish *Don Bueso*, concentration of the story goes hand in hand with superb lyrical touches, as so frequently in balladry.

Turning to our own ballads, we find subjects of romance treated there. The authors of *King Orfeo* and *Hind Horn* obviously knew the verse romances of *Sir Orfeo* and *Horn and Rymenhild*, but the leisurely movement of these romances was alien to the spirit of ballad narrative. Thus the poignant description of the terror of Orfeo's queen when she realized that she was in the power of the fairies, the delicate descriptions of her singing in the orchard, and of Orfeo's melancholy woodland life were compressed by the ballad poet, just as he reduced the magic intensity and the uncanny overtones of the description of the other world. In the same way the author of *Hind Horn* omits all unnecessary antecedents in the lives of his hero and heroine, and the seven opening stanzas set the story going without regard to purely decorative detail, but with strictest attention to essentials. The climax of *Hind Horn*, the recognition by means of the ring, occupies three rhyming couplets, two of them consisting of conversation, while the last couplet of the Scottish version concentrates into its two lines the significance of the story:

The red gowd shined oure them aw,
And the bride frae the bridegroom was stown awa.

Even more alien to the spirit of the ballads were the Arthurian romances of the Middle Ages, with their use of a very
deliberate technique of intricately constructed narrative,
inspired in its method by medieval rhetoricians. Arthurian
ballads are extant in this country and in Spain, but they do not
tell of the involved adventures of Lancelot and Perceval, or of
the Quest of the Grail. Instead we have simple episodes, such
as *The Boy and the Mantle* (Child, No. 29), reminiscent of the
ancient Irish version of the story, or single straightforward
adventure, such as *The Marriage of Sir Gawain* (Child, No. 31),
where comparison with other non-popular medieval versions
shows the author's extraordinary economy in telling a single
adventure shorn of incidentals. In Spanish Arthurian ballads
this conscious selection goes even further. *Lanzarote del Lago*, a
true ballad, however late in origin, compresses an adventure of
Lancelot's into fifty-five lines with quite extraordinary felicity,
and with a feeling for the supernatural reminiscent of our *Tam
Lin* or of the Danish *Sir Oluf*, while the eighteen lines of the
ballad of *Tristan de Leonis* achieve a poignancy closely related to
the pathos of the Scottish *Rare Willie drowned in Yarrow*, though
quite unlike the accounts of Tristan's death in the prose
romances on which it is based.

It has been shown that the ballad poet, with his gift for
compression, ignores the antecedents of his characters. The
vicissitudes of biographical development cannot be coerced
into the limits of the ballad, where the climax of a sharp and
sudden conflict between characters counts for everything, and
the antecedents and motivations of such conflicts for infinitely
less. We do not know precisely why the mistress of Lord
Randal poisons her lover. We have no idea what lies behind
the wonderful opening of *The Dowy Houms O Yarrow*:

> Late at een, drinkin the wine,
>   Or early in a mornin,
> They set a combat them between
>   To fight it in the dawning.

But we willingly accept the facts because we move in a poetic form defined by the immediacy of story-telling. Ballad heroes and heroines are committed to action for good or ill. They act freely and spontaneously, and their action defines the quality of balladry. That such action involves them again and again in tragic situations has its cause in the essentially unsentimental temper of the ballad, in the deep realization of the ballad poet that strife and struggle in human relationships lead to irretrievable loss and sorrow.

Nor is this preponderantly tragic attitude at odds with the pervasive lyrical element of the ballad. While there will be occasion further on to discuss the ballad refrain in this connexion, even within the ballad proper comparison and description rarely exist for their own sakes, divorced from the spirit of the whole. Comparisons are rarely of elaborate length, or strikingly original, and descriptions are brief and formalized. A sharp and intensely moving ballad like *Jamie Telfer in the Fair Dodhead* gains immeasurably by such lines as:

> The moon was up and the sun was down,
> 'T was the gryming of a new-fa'n snaw.

The Queen of Elfland's Nourice (Child, No. 40), which tells the poignant story of a mother forced to leave her own infant to become a nurse in the Elf-queen's family, stresses the tragedy that follows by two lovely introductory stanzas of lyrical power:

> I heard a cow low, a bonnie cow low,
>   An a cow low down in yon glen;
> Lang, lang will my young son greet
>   Or his mither bid him come ben.
>
> I heard a cow low, a bonnie cow low,
>   An a cow low down in yon fauld;
> Lang, lang will my young son greet
>   Or his mither take him frae cauld.

Thus one must agree with W. P. Ker that the fusion of tragic attitude and of lyrical intensity, concentrated on a critical event, constitutes the essential form of the ballad and distinguishes it from epic, romance, and non-narrative folk-song.

There are, however, other characteristics more often than not related to the exigencies of the ballad-form. British ballads in particular gain in compactness by the specific way in which they treat the conflict between two contrasting worlds. In the ballads dealing with supernatural motives this treatment is clear at first glance. *Clark Colven* opens with three stanzas which, for all the uneasiness in the conversation of the hero and his 'gay ladie,' are very much of the natural world, where lovers walk in a green garden, and a belt costs fifteen crowns and has to be paid for in hard cash. But the 'wall o Stream' and the maiden who there afflicts her faithless lover with mortal illness point the contrast most effectively: the lonely forest, the primeval figure of the seductive Washer at the Well who brooks no unfaithfulness, and who changes into a fish when Clark Colven threatens her, are all part of a world where artificial gardens and hard cash have no meaning whatsoever. To complete a movement as deft in its sequence of contrast as Andrew Marvell's *Coy Mistress*, the ballad moves back to an entirely realistic death-bed scene. Stanzas four and twelve of our ballad, linking the three stages of the narrative, show that the change from the natural world to the supernatural and back to the natural was perfectly conscious. *Clark Colven* is perhaps exceptional in the artistry with which it contrasts the two worlds, but the ballads dealing with ghosts draw much of their effect from a similar contrast. In *The Wife of Usher's Well*, where the central situation is put before us as quickly as possible, the depth of feeling aroused depends largely on the contrast between the cold world of the dead, who will not eat of the supper prepared by their mother, but who must hurry back where "the channerin worm doth chide," and the warm tenderness of the mother. The two worlds touch upon each other for a short while during the watches of the long November night, and in the two best versions of the ballad the hopelessness of the mother, which is the emotional tenor of the world of the quick, as submissiveness to supernatural forces is that of the world of her dead sons, is somewhat relieved. The farewell of the sons seems to establish a new order of things, an order which will not again be disturbed by the mother's despair; and the supremely disciplined stanza

> "I wish the wind may never cease,
>   Nor fashes in the flood,
> Till my three sons come hame to me,
>   In earthly flesh and blood"

is not the note on which the ballad closes. From a farewell to the mother, a farewell to the familiar places of barn and byre, the last stanza progresses to the intolerably poignant image of the bonny lass who, now that the dead sons must leave, is the pledge of quick life in the house of excessive grief, and thus places in due proportion the sudden intrusion into this life of the world of death. But the two worlds, merged into each other, contrasted, reconciled, or torn asunder for ever, occur in other ballads. In almost every case no special introduction is given. Conflict between certain groups of individuals is taken for granted within the poetic form of the ballad. The world of the bride's or the bridegroom's family and the world of the lovers, in their sentiments of authority and love respectively, are contrasted in such ballads as *Earl Brand*, *Clerk Saunders*, and *The Cruel Brother*, and the hatred of the bride's brothers for the bridegroom, in the choice of whom they were not consulted, needs no motivation. It is an emotion accepted for poetic purposes by the ballad poet and his public. The psychological motive is nothing; the sudden clash brought about by the contrast between the world of authority and the world of love is everything. The same insistence on the clash of two attitudes appears in dramatic vividness in ballads of outlaws and reivers as the clash between the world of the outlaw, with his own moral codes, and the world of civic law and order.

The central importance of this clash of values is enhanced by the impersonal attitude to his story of the ballad poet, who commonly leaves the hearer to draw his own conclusions. Pity, compassion, and horror are rarely forced upon the reader by an explicit statement, even though at times one may sense where

the poet's sympathies lie. The following are examples of a
very common ending:

> There was nae mean made for that lady,
>   In bowr where she lay dead.
>
> (Lord Ingram and Chiel Wyet)
>
> There was nae pity for that lady,
>   For she lay cald and dead,
> But a' was for him, Glenkindie,
>   In bower he must go mad.
>
> (Glasgerion)
>
> Nae meen was made for this young knight,
>   In bower where he lay slain,
> But a' was for sweet Maisry bright,
>   In fields where she ran brain.
>
> (Willie and Lady Maisry)

Such endings do not serve as more than a conclusion: they do
not cater for morbid sensibility. By being impersonal and
objective the ballad gains enormously. The emotional implications of *Sir Patrick Spens* are shown by description of action,
not by reflection. When Sir Patrick receives the summons to
an impossible task we are told that

> The first line that Sir Patrick red,
>   A loud lauch lauched he;
> The next line that Sir Patrick red,
>   The teir blinded his ee.

and, when his expedition has come to its fatal end, we hear:

> O, lang, lang may the ladies stand,
>   Wi thair gold kems in their hair,
> Waiting for their ain deir lords,
>   For they'll se thame na mair.

Dido looking from the Carthaginian shore for Æneas is no
more poignant a figure.

Closely related to this objectivity of the traditional ballad is
its dramatic power, a natural basis for poetry dealing with conflicts of opposed interests. Some of our finest ballads, *Edward*
and *Lord Randal* among them, consist entirely of highly
dramatic dialogue employing conversation of a stylized

character with consummate success. Even less successful
ballads, as *The False Knight upon the Road* or *The Maid freed from
the Gallows* (Child, Nos. 3, 95), which consist of dialogue, show
this same dramatic tendency. In many other ballads narrative
and dialogue are skilfully combined, so that the compression
of the narrative requires the hearer to co-operate with the
singer or reciter by filling in gaps with the help of his imagination. Again, *Sir Patrick Spens* is an outstanding example. In
the best version the warning of the sailor:

> "Late late yestreen I saw the new moone,
>   Wi the auld moone in hir arme,
> And I feir, I feir, my deir master,
>   That we will cum to harme."

is followed immediately by:

> O our Scots nobles were richt laith
>   To weet their cork-heild schoone;
> Bot lang owre a' the play wer playd,
>   Thair hats they swam aboone.

We are not even told whether the catastrophe overtook them
on the voyage out or on the voyage back, and it is interesting
that in two other versions (Child, B and G) the abruptness of
the transition in the version quoted is diluted by at least four
explanatory stanzas, powerful in themselves but tending to
detract from the final catastrophe.

In *Thomas Rhymer* we find the same principle of compression
at work. The Queen of Elfland and Thomas Rhymer set out
on their journey to Faery:

> For forty days and forty nights
>   He wade thro red blude to the knee
> And he saw neither sun nor moon
>   But heard the roaring of the sea.

Narrative economy, the compression of a whole world of terror
and strangeness, could scarcely go further. This technique of
the ballad by which the focus is rapidly shifted from one scene
to another has been rightly compared with the technique of the
cinema.[1]

[1] Cp. M. J. C. Hodgart, *The Ballads*, pp. 27-30.

On the formal side one of the most obvious features of the traditional ballad is its tendency towards repetition of phrases, so that verses and half-stanzas are repeated in the same ballad or even transferred to different ballads. This feature of repetition seems to fulfil two different purposes: within one and the same ballad it helps to knit the ballad together and serves as an obvious help to memory; secondly—and this applies particularly to repetition of epithets such as "bonnie," "fair," "sweet," and to the repetition of stock comparisons, "as green as any grass," "as white as morning milk"—it offered the ballad poet the continuity of a poetic tradition in which he could move conveniently. These stock comparisons and stock epithets really amount to what in eighteenth-century poetry we should call 'poetic diction.' Nor is it probable that the ballad poets considered them in a different light: to call a ballad heroine 'sweet,' even if her actions belied the epithet, or to call a hero of more than ordinary violence 'bonnie,' was required by the general temper of the ballad which, like all true folk-art, and especially like the folk-tale (which uses similar stereotyped epithets and comparisons), moved in a world in which the behaviour of hero and heroine, villain and victim, took place within certain limits of expected conduct, so that similar epithets could be applied to men and women in similar circumstances. But ballads retain sufficient interest in individual character and in individual plot to make the charge of uniformity ridiculous. Earl Brand and Clerk Saunders, Adam Bell and Robin Hood, Lord Barnard and Old Robyn of Portyngale, in spite of similarities in the narrative and in their conduct, differ sufficiently to make them stand out as individuals, and there is clearly only one Patrick Spens and only one Mary Hamilton.

With regard to the form of the ballad, there existed for the ballad poet certain accepted metres, dictated in the main by musical considerations, and developed from the metrical forms of the medieval French carols and dance lyrics. Ballad metres vary considerably, but they vary within certain limits of length of line and length of stanza; extremes are, on the whole, avoided. The four-line stanza, composed of alternating four-

and three-beat lines, with or without refrain, gives us the
traditional metre, as in:

> The horse Fair Annet rode upon
> He ambled like the wind,
> With silver he was shod before,
> With burning gold behind.

Usually only the second and fourth lines rhyme. This stanza-
form is capable of great variation, in accordance with the tune
of the ballad. There is no strict rule of alternating an accented
with an unaccented syllable or vice versa; half-accents and
hypermetric syllables are constantly found; musical considerations override regularity; but, on the other hand, the
four-line stanza remains a clearly recognizable form, eminently
suitable for compressed narrative.

As might be suspected in a form of poetry with such strong
lyrical tendencies, traditional ballads are rich in lines of high
poetic quality, quite apart from the power of their refrain or the
lyrical effect of the whole poem. The last stanza of *Bonnie
Willie Macintosh*,

> "Bonnie Willie Macintosh,
> Where now is your men?"
> "I left them in the Stapler,
> Sleeping in their sheen,"

has a compression and intensity that rivals the greatest lyrical
poetry. The lines from *Sir Patrick Spens*,

> Late late yestreen I saw the new moone,
> Wi the auld moone in hir arme,

partake of the same imaginative power as Coleridge's famous
stanza about the moon in *The Ancient Mariner*. Two lines like
these, from *Sheath and Knife*,

> The hawk had nae lure, and the horse had nae master,
> And the faithless hounds thro the woods ran faster

concentrate tragic emotion in unforgettable images. Wordsworth's greatest lines are matched by the poignancy of

The stalk is withered dry, my love,
So will our hearts decay.

(The Unquiet Grave)

and any poet would be proud of this image from a version of
The Wife of Usher's Well:

Then she made up a supper so neat,
As small, as small, as a yew-tree leaf.

Again and again ballad poetry achieves this concentration of
image and emotion in lines which occur even in ballads in no
way remarkable for emphasis on the more general lyrical
element.

A word must be said in this section about the refrain, the
recurring line at the end of a ballad stanza, so frequently a
characteristic of traditional ballads both in these islands and
abroad. Much ink has been spent on the problem of the
function of the refrain, and scholars have drawn attention to
certain musical considerations and to the probable importance
of the musical structure of the ballad in this respect. In the case
of some ballads there is justification for the view confirmed by
the practice of ballad-singing in the past, and by the evidence of
Danish balladry, that the narrative portion of the ballad fell to
the lot of an individual singer, professional or amateur, and
that the refrain was sung by the listening community or by the
dancers encircling the singer. The descent of early traditional
ballads from the carol, a non-narrative dance lyric with refrain,
makes such an explanation of the ballad refrain even more
probable. Furthermore, ballad refrains resemble the refrains
of carols in their emphasis on natural imagery, a feature of
Danish ballads also. Country scenery is often outlined with a
certainty of touch akin to Wordsworth's best lines or the deft
brush-strokes of a Constable. Refrains like

The broom blooms bonnie and so is it fair

(Leesome Brand)

And the norlan flowers spring bonny

(Sir Lionel)

And she saw the leaves growing green, my luve,

(The King's Dochter Lady Jean)

Come bend and bear away the boughs of yew
                    (*The Cruel Mother*)
As the dew flies over the mulberry tree.
                    (*The Wife wrapt in Wether's Skin*)

have an immediate lyrical appeal in their own right. It is
difficult to decide in many cases whether a ballad refrain is
in any demonstrable sense related to the ballad, as the words
of refrains are frequently corrupted in transmission. Thus

                    As the dove flies over the mulberry tree.
becomes
                    As the dew flies over the mulberry tree.
                    (*The Wife wrapt in Wether's Skin*)

and a perfectly natural image becomes strangely transfigured,
with a gain in imaginative power if not in logic. At other times
the appropriateness of a given refrain seems beyond question,
for no easily perceptible reason. In one version of *The Twa
Sisters* the first stanza runs:

        There was twa sisters in a bowr,
          Edinburgh, Edinburgh
        There was twa sisters in a bowr,
          Stirling for ay
        There was twa sisters in a bowr,
        There came a knight to be their wooer.
          Bonny Saint Johnston stands upon Tay.

How infinitely the stanza gains by the names of the Scottish
towns of the refrain, the repetition of the narrative verse, and
the delay in informing the listeners of the progress of the story!
This is subtly compensated by the refrain, which seems so
extraordinarily compelling. The whole stanza and every suc-
ceeding one culminates in what beyond all historical and geographical reality is the evocation of a walled city on the banks
of its swiftly flowing river. There is, one feels, a curious,
indefinable appropriateness that asserts itself in the same way in
The Cruel Brother (Child, No. 49), where the refrains of a ballad,
ferocious and tragic in character, by their evocation of flowers
and natural colour seem to serve as an artistically brilliant
counterpoint:

There was three ladies played at the ba,
  With a hey ho and a lillie gay
There came a knight and played oer them a'
  As the primrose spreads so sweetly

Or in another version:

A gentleman cam oure the sea,
  Fine flowers in the valley
And he has courted ladies three,
  With the light green and the yellow

In these ballads the joyous notes of the refrains balance the
sombreness of the main narrative, and in this contrast lies the
appropriateness of many of the best refrains. Furthermore,
because of its repetition, the refrain more than any feature
stresses the lyrical aspect of the ballad. The tragic temper, the
dramatic compression, and the tenseness of ballad-narrative
seem refined in the refrain. Ballads like *The Cruel Brother* and
Lord Randal, which might otherwise overwhelm us with the
starkness of their tragedy, are lifted by their refrains on to an
æsthetically more compelling plane, where disinterested
experience becomes possible.

IV

Many of our traditional ballads are not found outside Britain.
The Robin Hood ballads, on the one hand, and such Border
ballads as *Johnie Armstrong* or *Jamie Telfer in the Fair Dodhead*
on the other, are clearly restricted to England and Scotland
respectively. But even traditional ballads of a non-historical
character are sometimes found in Britain only. Thus, *The
Unquiet Grave* has not been found outside England, while *Tam
Lin*, *Sir Patrick Spens*, and *Clerk Saunders* seem exclusively
Scottish. Other British ballads, mainly those in which historical events do not play an important part, are found in the
United States; sometimes, as in *Little Musgrave and Lady
Barnard*, *Lady Isabel and the Elf-knight*, *Lord Randal*, and others,
in very numerous and interesting versions. But a considerable
number of our traditional ballads enjoy international currency,

in the sense that many Continental ballads resemble British ballads in plot, treatment, turn of phrase, and often in melody. Nor is such resemblance due to the simple descent of Continental versions from British ones or vice versa. The problem is more complex, as may be seen from the following illustrations.

The ballad of *Earl Brand* tells the story of a conflict of loyalties—a favourite subject of balladry, descended from great antiquity, and closely related to the old Norse Eddic songs of Helgi. A lady elopes with her lover and is pursued by her father and brothers, whom her lover attacks fiercely, slaying one after the other, until the lady invokes his mercy, as a result of which her lover receives a deadly wound from the last mortally stricken survivor of her family. The Scottish ballad is deeply moving, yet the sequence of events is not easy to make out. Now Child has drawn attention to a very fine Danish ballad, *Ribold and Guldborg*, which is clearly a congener (*i.e.*, ballad identical in subject-matter) of *Earl Brand*. In the Danish ballad, when the lover has slain all members of the lady's kin except her youngest brother, she calls her lover by name, imploring him to spare the youngest brother, and at that instant her lover receives a mortal wound. Told in this way, the ballad makes sense, for in ancient belief a man's name was intimately linked with the principle of life in him. Heroes of medieval romance conceal their identity from their enemy as zealously as Odysseus conceals his from Polyphemus. Knowledge of a man's name conveys power over his soul. The heroine of the Danish ballad, by calling the name of her lover under the stress of unendurable emotion, deprives him of a magical protection against her kin. As her lover has warned her against this emergency, the poignancy and essential tragedy of the ballad is greatly heightened. From our point of view the versions of this plot in British ballads make complete sense only with the help of the Danish ballad. To the central incident of the 'dead-naming' *Earl Brand* alludes in only three stanzas (incomprehensible except for the Danish parallel):

"If they come on me ane by ane,
I'll smash them a' down bane by bane

"If they come on me ane and a'
Ye soon will see my body fa'.

.   .   .   .

An bad her never change her cheer
Untill she saw his body bleed.

Here, something like an order for the lady to preserve silence is
dimly discernible. Only the Danish version makes the curious
allusion quite clear. On the other hand, *Earl Brand* preserves
an archaic feature of the original Scandinavian parent ballad
from which both Danish and Scottish versions must have
descended. Earl Brand and his lady are intercepted by a
mysterious figure, "ald Carl Hood, he's ay for ill, but he's
never for good." Now we know that the 'hooded one' is a
constant Scandinavian epithet for the pagan god of war,
Odhin, who wore a dark hood to hide the loss of an eye, given
in search of wisdom. Odhin, in Norse mythology, is the constant instigator of strife, as he wishes to gather all the fallen
warriors in a ghostly retinue round him. Thus, true to his
nature, he betrays Earl Brand's elopement, the mortal struggle
takes place, and "ald Carl Hood" himself gives Earl Brand a
treacherous wound. The Danish versions do not, as far as I
know, contain this final climax, completely in keeping with
Odhin's nature, and paralleled by his actions in the Eddic
Helgi songs from which the Danish and British versions are
descended. Thus Danish and British versions are mutually
illuminating. *Earl Brand* is only one of many examples where
Scandinavian parallels help us to understand British ballads.
Historical considerations make such contacts easily intelligible.

Quite apart from Scandinavian invasions, there was constant intercourse between Scotland and Scandinavia during
the Middle Ages, and the Scottish and Danish languages were
not altogether unlike. Sailors and fishermen from both sides
of the North Sea must have found it possible to enjoy each
other's songs. But many British ballads have congeners not

only in Scandinavia but all over Europe, sometimes even to the exclusion of Scandinavian parallels.

The ballad entitled by Child *Lady Isabel and the Elf-knight* has a bewildering currency all over Europe, from Norway to central Italy, from Brittany to Poland. The main plot of the young woman outwitting—or in some versions failing to outwit—a murderer, supernatural in some versions, entirely human in others, has been thought to originate in the Apocryphal story of Judith and Holofernes, influenced by the elf-lore of the North. Holland, from which one of the best versions of this ballad comes, has been claimed as the geographical centre from which all other versions ultimately derive. The lilting refrain of one Scottish version, "Aye as the gowans grow gay," its emphasis on the supernatural character of the villain, and the eerie location of other Scottish variants by the deserted seashore seem very far removed from the grim but perfectly natural atmosphere of certain German versions. Probably various motives have combined in different countries in varied proportions: we can discern the motive of Judith and Holofernes, of the highwayman in search of costly booty (there exists a fourteenth-century Italian short story very close to the ballad), and of the seductive power of music in the Scottish, Scandinavian, German, and other Continental versions. A full investigation of the ballad would probably show that each of these motives gave rise to separate ballads, which were later fused because they resembled each other in the central situation of a woman outwitting a pursuer.

The ballad of *The Maid freed from the Gallows*, in the best surviving British form, is told in a series of rapid dialogues between a girl about to be hanged and her father, mother, brother, and sister, whom she implores to ransom her from death, but who coldly refuse. In the end her lover appears, who agrees to ransom her. No reason for the girl's plight is given: we do not know whether she has committed some crime or is innocent. The true explanation of the ballad can only be found by looking at its Continental congeners, of which there are Sicilian, German, Scandinavian, and Slavonic examples. In nearly all these the girl is held to ransom by pirates, and this makes immediate sense. The ballad is clearly a comment on the triumph of love over possessiveness, the cause for the test of the strength of affection being provided by an emergency real enough for dwellers on the pirate-haunted shores of the Mediterranean or the Viking-infested waters of the North. Now, it is quite impossible to say whether the Sicilian example of this ballad, a very fine version known as *Scibilia Nobili*, or the one from the Faeroe Islands known as *Frisa Visa* (*i.e.*, the ballad of the Frisians, who had a bad reputation as pirates) is the original. We can say negatively that the Scottish versions, because of their obscurity of plot, are probably not.

Finally, *Lord Randal*, the extraordinarily moving ballad in dialogue of the young man poisoned by his sweetheart, presents us with an even more fascinating problem. This fine ballad, which seems at first so typically Scottish, "has been found," to quote Professor Gerould, "as far East as Czecho-Slovakia and Hungary, as far North as Scotland and Sweden and as far South as Calabria," and there are innumerable North American versions. We know that it was known in Italy over three hundred years ago, and it is worth while comparing in detail the Italian version, noted down in the middle of the nineteenth century, with the Scottish ballad. Not only does the Italian version agree with the Scottish ballad point for point in the dialogue treatment of the story and in the outline of the plot—the return of the poisoned youth to his mother, the questioning, the confessions of the visit to his sweetheart, the meal of eels or snakes and its effect on the dogs, the testament of the dying youth—but both versions show complete agreement as to the structural arrangement and the musical character of each stanza. To show this more clearly we give the Scottish and Italian versions in parallel columns:

Scottish (2nd stanza)	*Italian* (1st stanza)
"And wha met ye there Lord Randal, my son? And wha met you there My handsome young man?"	"Where have you been yesternight, My son, dear, handsome and wise? Where have you been yesternight?"

Scottish (2nd stanza)	*Italian* (1st stanza)
"O I met wi my true-love	"I have been at my lady's
Mother, mak my bed soon;	Mother, I am sick at heart,
For I am wearied wi hunting;	I have been at my lady's
And fain wad lie down."	Alas, I am dying, alas."

Structural agreement could scarcely go further, and the stylized and at the same time caressing address of the mother to her son in the Italian version is found with equal effect in another Scottish version, where the mother calls him tenderly "my jollie young man." That there may exist a close connexion between the English and Italian versions is indicated by the fact that the victim of the poisoning is called by the Italian-sounding names of Tiranti, Tyranty, and Teronto in certain North American versions, instead of Randal, or Roland. But quite apart from Italian, British, and American ballads, German, Scandinavian, and other versions show the same treatment of the ballad in plot, form, and essential structure; and, while the relation of poisoner, poisoned, and interrogator varies (sometimes a child is poisoned by his step-mother or grandmother, sometimes a husband, poisoned by a mistress, speaks to his wife) there can be no doubt that we deal with the same ballad, yet there is no clear way to tell where the ballad originated. A version from Lusatia, however, shows how a ballad can change for the worse. While this version still clings to the original structure of stylized dialogue, it tells the story of a boy poisoned, possibly without malice, through eating part of a fish caught in a neighbour's stable by being speared with a dung-fork. Not only is this version interesting because the poisoning is removed from the more intimate relationships of the other versions, but the catching of a fish in a stable shows how the ballad was adapted by the inhabitants of Lusatia to local conditions, with the curious amphibious fen-existence of the inhabitants of that region.

Where, as with many parallel ballads existing in different countries we deal with clear cases of borrowing and conscious imitation, the question of how ballads travelled from one country to the other is of special importance. Now it seems clear that in the past when ballad singing was a common accomplishment (as the humming of swing-tunes is now) ballads must have spread from country to country in a great variety of ways: sailors bringing wine from Bordeaux to English ports, pilgrims visiting shrines in strange lands, apprentices seeking experience abroad, artisans fleeing from religious persecution, minstrels, international by their very profession—all these doubtless helped to spread a knowledge of ballads. Attention has been drawn to *The Maid freed from the Gallows*, and it has been discovered that a Cumberland version of this ballad agrees in story and tune with a version from Westphalia. Now Southern Westphalia is ore-mining country, and between 1570 and 1590 German miners are known to have worked at Coniston and Keswick. This is just one illuminating instance which shows how the problem of kinship between ballads must be seen in relation to the general pattern of social life.

On the other hand, the study of ballads has shown that certain areas of Europe are more productive of ballads than others, and that if we plot the probable lines of dissemination of a particular ballad story and its tune we may find it radiating from one of these centres. This we may assume to be the place of origin, especially if the ballad, as it travels to the periphery of its area of dissemination, loses in distinctness. Thus in the case of the Sicilian version of *The Maid freed from the Gallows*, compared with the English, and in the case of the Scottish or Italian versions of *Lord Randal*, compared with the Lusatian, we can assert that certain versions of a ballad are inferior, because less consistent as a story than others, and similar considerations apply to ballad tunes. In comparing ballads on a large scale, scholars have therefore come to the conclusion that we can determine certain important centres for the dissemination of European balladry. The Scottish Border and Aberdeenshire in these islands, Jutland and Skane in Scandinavia, Piedmont in Italy, certain mountainous districts in Yugoslavia and Greece, the north-west and west of Spain are districts which seem to have been more productive of balladry than, say, the central Midlands or southern England, the valley of the Seine or Loire, or the hilly country of central Germany. The question then arises: are there historical and above all social conditions which favour the growth of traditional balladry? This problem will be considered in the next section, with particular reference to the English and Scottish traditional ballad.

V

In many ways the study of the social background of the ballad requires a preliminary discussion of the age of these poems. Changes in society clearly influence the creation and the popularity of specific forms of literary art. The novel requires reasonably cheap printing and a reading public of some education and sufficient leisure, the radio play technical and social developments of a different kind. But, while it is relatively simple to give accurate details as to the age of literary works, the traditional ballad, oral in transmission, and therefore independent of printing in its early stages, cannot be so easily dated. In the Middle Ages, when secular narrative poetry consisted largely of romances circulating in manuscript among the lords and ladies for whom they were written, authors did not consider the oral songs current among the people worthy of much notice. To authors familiar with the highly polished stories of courtly romance the compressed and crude forms sung by minstrels to a less refined audience must have seemed inept and barbarous, lacking in the careful composition, refinement of manners, and leisurely attention to detail by which medieval romances acquired their fame. William Langland (*circa* 1340–1400), more in sympathy with the people than with courtly society, makes it clear, in *Piers Plowman*, that by 1377 popular poems on Robin Hood and other outlaws were current among the people. But popular poems are not necessarily ballads, and we do not know whether these popular poems were, in fact, the ballads of Robin Hood, of which the earliest isolated manuscript is not earlier than

1450. Furthermore, Langland's reference is unique, and a single record does not supply evidence of the flourishing of traditional balladry before 1400 in this country. On the Continent it is thought that ballads came into their own in the course of the late fourteenth century (possibly somewhat earlier in Denmark), but no conclusions about British balladry can be drawn from this fact. Nor is it permissible to take the subject-matter of ballads as evidence of their age. The language, diction, and other features of many ballads show that existing versions cannot have been written contemporaneously with the events described. Ballads dealing with the battles of Otterburn (1388) and Harlaw (1411), for example, are generally thought to have come into existence at least fifty years after the date of these battles. E. K. Chambers has shown that *Queen Eleanor's Confession* cannot have been written, even in its original form, at the time of the Queen's death (1204). The ballad relates that the Queen's confession is heard by *two* friars: this almost necessarily precludes the composition of the ballad before the Reformation, since every Catholic would have known that confession can be heard by only one priest. For these reasons it is best to preserve an open mind on the question of the earliest date of British balladry. Evidence from the Continent, isolated manuscripts and references, suggest that British ballads may have been current about 1400, though we cannot be certain. There cannot be any doubt, however, that ballads flourished by the mid-sixteenth century, when references are so numerous as to suggest an origin considerably earlier than 1500. For this reason the evidence of *The Complaynt of Scotland* (1549) is of particular importance, as it establishes clear proof of the existence of traditional balladry.

The Complaynt is a pastoral poem written in that dialect of southern Scotland in which so many of our best ballads are preserved, and it gives a list of a number of ballads known to the author as current among the country people of southern Scotland. The list of ballads is interesting and repays study. The first 'ballad' mentioned is *the taylis of canterberrye*, perhaps a popular adaptation of Chaucer's *Canterbury Tales*, the loss of which amounts to a major literary catastrophe. Next we find an entry entitled *robene hude and litel ihone*, clearly a form of the ballad from the English Robin Hood cycle, which must have enjoyed popularity in Scotland, as we find another entry in *The Complaynt* relating to a dance of *Robene hude* in the section devoted to a list of dance-songs as opposed to narrative poems. Going back to the record of narrative poems, we find next a very puzzling entry, which in modern spelling reads: *How the King of Estmure Land married the King's daughter of Vestmure land*. E. K. Chambers suggests that this may be a Scottish version of the ballad of *King Estmere* (Child, No. 60), which has roots in Germanic epic tradition, but one wonders whether it should not be connected with the three fragmentary versions of the story of *Fause Foodrage* discussed below (pp. 53, 54). The next entry, *The Young Tamlene and of the Bold Braband*, may refer to the magnificent Scottish ballad *Tam Lin*, but unless Braband is a form of the heroine's name there seems little connexion. Songs of *The Battle of Harlaw* and *The Hunting of Cheviot* seem references to the historical ballads bearing these names. Finally we select the entry entitled *Ihonne Ermistrangis dance*, which must relate in some way to the Border hero, Johnie Armstrong, whose fate survives in ballad-form, and who was executed in 1530. After *The Complaynt* references to traditional ballads and the printing of ballad versions become fairly common, so that in the date of *The Complaynt* (1549), apart from a few specific instances of earlier references, we have the first clear-cut proof of the flourishing of traditional balladry.

Now, simply as a matter of statistics, it is interesting to find that the regions of the Scottish Border and of the Lowlands are responsible for a considerable proportion of our balladry, and, in view of the dependence of literature on social environment, we may be entitled to suggest that the social characteristics of these areas during the late Middle Ages and up to about 1700, especially the lack of exaggerated differences between feudal and agricultural classes, made it possible for such a ballad tradition to arise there. The suggestion that the traditional ballad grew up in a homogeneous agricultural and feudal

environment in which most of its stories are set is likely for a
variety of reasons. In the villages opportunities for communal gatherings, as fairs, harvest festivals, sheep-shearing,
and spinning on long winter nights provided scope for the
professional or amateur reciter to entertain the community
with verse narratives based on literary sources, on commonly
held beliefs, or on incidents of a dramatic nature relating to
their district or a neighbouring one. The social cleavage
between villager and squire or laird was not so marked in the
late Middle Ages and the Renaissance period as in the eighteenth and nineteenth centuries, certainly not in Scotland, and
the entertainment of the laird and his lady consisted frequently
enough in the singing or hearing of the same ballads that
delighted the villagers. From Denmark, with its astonishingly
vigorous ballad tradition, we know that during the period in
question the poorer nobility and yeomen delighted in the singing of ballads, and that listening to their recital constituted the
main part of leisure-hour entertainment. Ballads were preserved there in aristocratic families, collected in song-books,
and sung at social gatherings. The first printed collection of
Danish ballads (the *Kæmpe Viser* of 1591) was published by
the Danish humanist Vedel at the request of Queen Sophia of
Denmark, who had been entertained by him and his friend, the
great astronomer Tycho Brahe, with the singing of ballads,
when in autumn 1586 she had been storm-stayed for some days
at Tycho's famous island observatory. The position in the
Scottish Lowlands in the sixteenth and seventeenth centuries
was similar, and collections of ballads in the private song-
books of Scottish families have provided collectors, from the
eighteenth century onward, with many excellent versions of
our most cherished ballads.

But a specific social environment is only half the story. The
other half is provided by the existence, in the Border districts
and in the Lowlands, of the social and human tensions that
provide incidents for the ballad-maker's imagination. For life
in the 'debateable lands' on both sides of the Border and in the
Lowlands was precarious enough up to 1745. The cattle-raids

and robberies of moss-trooper and reiver in the dales of the Border, especially between 1500 and 1570, created situations in plenty which called for the exercise of courage, self-reliance, and sturdy manhood. The epic quality of such ballads as *Johnie Armstrong*, *Jock o the Side*, and many others reminds one insistently of the true epic grandeur of the Old Irish *Cattle Raid of Cooley*, and the reivers of the dales partake in no small measure of the qualities of the Irish hero Cuchullainn and his comrades. For the Irish heroes and for the Scottish moss-trooper cattle were the most important unit of economy. Whatever the legal or moral rights and wrongs of the specific case, the cut and thrust of the situation as such lent itself to memorable narrative poetry based on grim economic realities. The high heroic spirit of *The Hunting of the Cheviot*, where raiding was still a national pastime rather than an affair of individuals, is still strong and compulsive in these later ballads. Again, the political troubles of the Lowlands, with their rivalry of contending clans in the sixteenth and seventeenth centuries, provided the sense of social tension by which balladry grows. Ballads like *Lord Maxwell's Last Goodnight*, *Bonnie James Campbell*, and many others are based on these rivalries, and their elegiac power results from the poet's consciousness of the tragic implications of the social situation. This consciousness enables him to deal with violent and cruel actions, as in *Edom o Gordon* or *The Fire of Frendraught*, without recourse to sensationalism. The additional tension between Highlands and Lowlands acted likewise as a stimulus for balladry, so that ballads of abductions and violent love-matches, such as *Bonnie Baby Livingston* or *Rob Roy*, gain in strength by being related to the conflicts inherent in the situation of the Highland-Lowland region. It seems clear, then, that the social tensions implicit in the history of Southern Scotland acted as perhaps the most important single stimulus for the continuing growth of sixteenth- and seventeenth-century balladry in this area. Comparison with the situation in England suggests that the greater political stability and the more rapid growth of mercantile and industrial enterprise

south of the Border did not offer traditional balladry as much
scope as the essentially feudal and agricultural situation in the
North. It may be argued that this emphasis on the Border and
the Lowlands as centres of British balladry is specious, since
in Scotland ballad-collecting began at a time when ballads were
still widely sung, while in England it began only towards the
end of the nineteenth century, when it was almost too late, but
when, in spite of adverse conditions, many valuable ballad
versions were recovered. Ballad-collecting started so early in
Scotland because there were so many good ballads to be
found, and because, as late as the eighteenth century, Scottish
life provided situations and conflicts that could become the
subject-matter of new and vigorous ballads. In spite of the
absence of such situations south of the Border, the older
traditional ballads continued to be sung, but Southern balladry
lacked the hard, more tragic, and in a sense more realistic qualities of the Scottish ballads, which were born out of the specific
situations of seventeenth- and eighteenth-century Scotland.

Mention has been made of the fact that the social situation
in Denmark, where ballads were cultivated by the lesser
nobility and yeomanry as the principal form of literary entertainment, resembled the situation in Scotland. Some of the best
Danish ballads reflect incidents in the life of these classes
similar to those in Scottish and English balladry. The long
Danish ballad of *Marsk Stige* has clearly attracted material, such
as the seduction of Marsk Stige's wife by the young king, and
the curious encounter of Marsk with the elf-woman, originally
unconnected with the central plot of Marsk's rebellion against
King Eric Klipping. But Marsk's banishment and his setting
up as a pirate on the island of Hjelm remind one of the out-
lawed Johnie Armstrong's existence in the fastnesses of the
Border, at loggerheads with royal power. The Danish
peasant's complaint at Marsk's lawlessness

> The goodman goes to the field abroad,
>   And for to sow his corn,
> And ever he prays "God send us help,
>   Since Hjelm has gotten a horn."

calls to mind Jamie Telfer's plight, as his peaceful existence is disturbed by lawless robbery. In the same way the conversation of Niels Ebbeson, the hero of another famous Danish ballad, with his brother-in-law, who attempts to prevent Niel's escape after the murder of Count Gerard of Holstein, stresses a conception of loyalty reminiscent of the spirit of the conversations between Robin Hood and members of his band in the English ballads. Some of the finest Danish ballads, therefore, relating to the fate of the lesser nobility or yeomanry in times of stress and conflict, resemble closely British ballads on similar themes.

In Spain also we find the dependence of balladry on the impact of specific political factors and on the tensions implicit in a mixed feudal and agricultural community. For the purposes of this discussion it is immaterial that Spanish ballads telling of the internecine warfare among the Spanish nobles or of the struggle against the Moors, under the leadership of the Cid, derive from epic sources. These ballads remain essentially the songs of the lesser nobility, fighting each other, fighting the Moors, or asserting their independence against the unjustified encroachments of royal power. This spirit is seen in the superb ballads of the *Infantes of Lara*, and in many of the Cid ballads. It is strikingly similar to the spirit of British and Danish ballads in such jewels of the Spanish *romancero* as *Bernardo del Carpio refuses Carpio to the King* or *El Infante Vengador*. Bernardo del Carpio, summoned to appear in the royal presence to answer charges of treason, calls to his side his retainers, just as Johnie Armstrong and Robin Hood do.

> Four hundred men of my household
> Who eat my bread in my hall,
> A hundred shall go to Carpio
> To guard my castle and wall.
> A hundred shall watch the highroads
> Lest anyone pass by the way.
> Two hundred of them go with me,
> With the king I'll have my say.
> If ill he intends against me
> He shall have from us worse play.

And, as Robin Hood's men are ready to rescue their leader at
the call of his horn, so Bernardo's men are ready when the
King threatens their leader, and Bernardo has only to call

> "To my side, to my side, my two hundred
>   Who eat my bread in my hall
> For the day has come, my retainers,
>   When we must gain honour all."

and the King, like his English counterpart or the Bishop of
Hereford, is glad to make the threat appear a jest. Clearly
Bernardo del Carpio is a noble while Robin Hood is only a
yeoman (in the genuine tradition, at least), but the similarities
in the stress on implicit loyalty are of greater importance than
the differences in social status.

Various regions of Spain were frontier country in the Middle
Ages, as a consequence of the gradual expulsion of the Moors.
Thus, both politically and socially, Spain was in a position not
unlike that prevailing on the Scottish Border or in the border
country between Highlands and Lowlands. Moorish invasions
differed only in degree from the Anglo-Scottish troubles, and
from the raids of the Lords of the Isles and their clansmen,
while the similarity of personal problems arising in both
countries extended even to minor features. The groups of
Spanish ballads known significantly as 'ballads of the frontier'
and 'Moorish ballads' have suffered from sentimental dis-
tortion and literary imitation, yet one cannot help noticing the
similarity between the tragic version of *Bonny Baby Livingston*
and one of the Spanish versions of the *Romance de Moriana*. In
one case a Lowland girl is abducted from her sweetheart by
Highland raiders to be forced into marriage with a man whose
language she does not speak. In the other a Christian lady is
captured by Moors on Midsummer Day to become the wife of
a Moorish lord. Bonny Baby Livingston dies heartbroken in
Glenlion's Highland keep, while her lover stands helpless at the
gate. Moriana, faithful to her Christian lover, is led to execution while he stands by, powerless, among the spectators.

Thus in many Spanish ballads we find almost the same social

setting and the same response to specific situations of political
strain and stress as in the Scottish ballads.

Much the same is true of the great body of Yugoslav
balladry, where, in an agricultural and feudal setting of great
homogeneity, the ballad flourished considerably as a result of
political tension: the deeds of the central hero, Marko Kral-
jevic (akin in many ways to the Cid and to the heroes of the
Scottish Border), and the invasion of the Turks during the
fourteenth century supply the ballads with perhaps their
greatest subject-matter. The ballad of the fate of the Jugovici
brothers and their mother, one of a magnificent cycle dealing
with the deadly struggle of the Serbs against the Turks, rises to
a tragic pitch which relates it to the Spanish ballad of *The
Infantes of Lara* or to our *Johnie Armstrong*. But the social setting of the Jugovici ballad, as of *The Infantes of Lara*, or of our
best English and Scottish ballads, is feudal only in the sense
that it tells of the fate of men and women of a slightly higher
social rank than that of the hearers of the ballad: the tenor of
life, its values, its moral problems are of the kind immediately
intelligible to the members of the rural communities, dependent, both politically and economically, on the lesser nobility.
It seems probable, then, that traditional balladry not only
thrives best in such a mixed feudal and agricultural society, and
preferably in a border region subject to political or social
tension, but that its origins must be discerned in a past when
this pattern of society was of outstanding importance in the
life of the national community. In this way the Border and
the Lowlands seem closely related to such other ballad centres
as the valleys and mountain passes of Northern Spain and
Serbia; and Anglo-Scottish troubles and the internecine
struggles of Scottish clans are akin to the Spanish struggles
against the Moors, and the agony of the Serbian Empire in its
struggle against the Turks.

The break-up of feudal and agricultural communities by
industrialization, the growth of cities, and the development of
bigger national units all over Europe hastened the decline of
the ballad. On the other hand ballads continued to flourish up

to comparatively recent times where there existed the appro-
priate social and political climate for their growth. Thus a fine
body of new balladry was created by Yugoslav popular
minstrels as a result of the wars against the Turks in the first
decades of the nineteenth century. The best of these ballads
rival the great songs which sprang up as a result of similar
social and political conditions in the fourteenth century, when
the Serbian Empire bled to death on the Field of the Black-
birds (Kossovo), and its Czar Lazar had to choose between the
earthly glory of victory and the heavenly glory of martyrdom,
as is recorded in one of the greatest of all ballads. In the same
way Russian peasant minstrels round the shores of Lake
Onega, American backwoodsmen in the remote valleys of the
Appalachians, and even railroadmen and lumberjacks in the
mid-Western states of the U.S.A. created new ballads until
quite recently. The singing of old ballads, on the other hand,
as among the Spanish Jews in South-eastern Europe, may
linger on even when the conditions for the creation of new
ballads are no more. Having defined the type of community in
which traditional balladry flourishes, and the stimulus it seems to
require for its growth, we shall find our conclusions of help in
discussing the problems of ballad variation and authorship.

VI

We have, up to now, referred to ballads in much the same
way as we would speak of individual poems of literary character such as Keats's *Ode to a Grecian Urn*, Tennyson's *In Memo-
riam*, or Edith Sitwell's *Still falls the Rain*. We must now
qualify our remarks in one important respect: ballads are
essentially oral poetry meant to be sung or recited and heard,
and not to be written down in books and read. Now when
ballads came to be written down in the eighteenth and early
nineteenth centuries, scholars quickly realized that the text of a
ballad recorded in one village often differed materially from the
text of the same ballad written down in another village not
many miles away. The main outline of the story might be

essentially the same in both cases and variations occur in phrases only, or one version might be fuller or more complex in its treatment of the plot, or the resemblance of the two forms of the ballad might be restricted to the main features of the plot. In every case scholars were faced with the question: which of these versions or variants is the authentic ballad? Or, alternatively: is there such a thing as the authentic ballad in the sense in which we speak of the authentic text of a literary poem? There are many variants of *Edward, The Wife of Usher's Well*, and *Mary Hamilton*. In each variant the essential story of the ballad is the same. In each the story develops logically, and we cannot dismiss any of the variants given as inferior to any other on the ground that it shows a misunderstanding or a clumsy interpretation of the original plot. Nor are there any good grounds for discriminating on grounds of artistic excellence, not a very safe criterion at the best of times, as an earlier form may be inferior or superior to a later form. Thus, is the so-called B version of *Edward* (p. 101) really superior to A? It is, on the whole, more familiar, but that is not quite the same thing. Stanza seven of A:

> "What about did the plea begin,
>   Son Davie, son Davie?"
> "It began about the cutting of a willow wand
>   That would never been a tree."

flashes across our mind the picture of a fratricidal quarrel as compelling as anything in the familiar stanzas of version B. However, the case of *Edward* is relatively simple, as scholars have shown linguistic reasons for believing that the B version was rewritten by an eighteenth-century author with literary skill.[1] But, in *The Wife of Usher's Well*, it seems impossible to choose between

> The cock he hadna crawd but once,
>   And clappd his wings at a',
> When the youngest to the eldest said,
>   Brother we must awa'

(Version A)

[1] Cp. M. J. C. Hodgart, *The Ballads*, p. 102 f.

and

> O the young cock crew in the merry Linkem,
>   And the wild fowl chirpd for day;
> The aulder to the younger did say,
>   Dear brother, we maun away.
>
>   (*Version B*)

But perhaps the two most famous versions of *Mary Hamilton* (there are many more) show the complexity of the problem even more clearly. Is version A (the one chosen by us, pp. 205–207), for all the immediacy with which it starts and the poignancy with which it closes, really superior, and, if superior in any demonstrable sense, more original than B, with its two careful introductory stanzas—of which the first seems to end with a brilliantly ironical line, and its final sharply pointed conversation between Mary and her seducer? Version A contains such a perfect stanza as:

> Down then cam the auld queen,
>   Goud tassels tying her hair:
> "O Marie, where's the bonnie wee babe
>   That I heard greet sae sair?"

but B compensates by the Queen's speech:

> "O rise, O rise, Mary Hamilton,
>   Arise, and go with me;
> There is a wedding in Glasgow town
>   This day we'll go and see."

For that matter, who would choose between the white robes of A and the golden ones, of B or Mary's speech to her parents in either version?

Establishment of an older variant or of a variant closer to the original on purely æsthetic grounds is not merely difficult, as we have seen; it is not merely unwise, as a ballad may obviously flower into beauty at any time in the course of its chequered history; it is, in fact, impossible, since we judge by standards of literary poetry, which too often overlook the exigencies of oral recitation. It is safer to base judgment on consistency of plot, but even that criterion is of help in a relatively small number of ballads only, and enables us to construct merely the skeleton of the archetypal ballad. Examples of real inconsistency like that of *Sir Lionel*, analysed by Professor Gerould in his suggestive book, *The Ballad of Tradition*, are rare. Therefore an example in which inconsistency of plot helps to establish the outline of the original ballad story may be welcome. In variant A of *Fause Foodrage* (Child, No. 89) we are told of three royal wooers of a lady, but after the first stanza the two unsuccessful wooers are not heard of again. The murderer of the lady's husband is neither of the two, but a rebel freshly introduced for that purpose. The rest of the ballad—the escape of the Queen, the touching exchange of children, the loyal subject and his wife, the revenge for the murder by the hand of the young prince—though told with great spirit, is completely unconnected with the opening stanza. If we now turn to variant B we can be certain that we are dealing with another version of the same ballad; the names of the three wooers are almost identical, the reasons for their wooing, the failure of the first two kings, and the success of the third correspond to what we know from A; but the exchange of the children, similar in detail to A, is due to the threat of one rejected wooer, who has murdered his successful rival and is slain by the young prince in revenge. Thus B links up the wooing and the latter part of the ballad, at any rate as far as one of the unsuccessful wooers is concerned, but compared with A it fails in not explaining how the young prince comes to realize his position. Thus neither A nor B gives the whole story; in the case of A comparison of our ballad with a related Scandinavian ballad (*Svend of Voldeslov*) even suggests that the story of the three wooers has been contaminated by another story. But we still have to deal with the four extraordinarily impressive stanzas of Child's variant of C: poetically superior because of their suggestiveness, they are clearly fragmentary, indicating the trend of the story of the ballad rather than developing it. C makes the Westmure King, whom B completely neglects, the assassin, but it endeavours to imply some development in the case of the Eastmure King. If we now look at the three variants in order to discover which one is closest to the original story, we must come to the conclusion that it is impossible to reconstruct the story in any detail. We find three wooers of a lady, two motivated by greed, the third by love; the murder of the successful wooer by one of the unsuccessful ones; a time of tribulation for the widowed queen; a final act of revenge. All these motifs are clearly pieces of the story-pattern, traditional in the sense that many a fine medieval story has been built up on the foundation of one or more of these motifs, but one cannot help feeling that all three variants derive from a definite tale irrecoverably lost, and that all speculation as to which of the three variants preserves the greatest number of features of this original story is idle in the extreme.

The test of consistency, if applied solely to the plot of a ballad, may thus help to establish the probable outline of the original ballad, especially if we remember that an older variant is not necessarily closer to the original. The memory of a more recent reciter, who has heard a more consistent version, may be more accurate than that of an earlier reciter, who may have tampered with the ballad or heard an inferior version. Consistency must be an objective criterion if it is to remain useful. We have seen that the artistic excellence of a ballad version is frequently a matter of subjective taste, in which the critic's standards of what is or is not a good poem tend to intrude. Therefore, the question of artistic excellence should not be combined with that of consistency in endeavouring to reconstruct an original ballad-form. For this reason the subtle arguments by which Archer Taylor establishes that the Scottish versions of *Edward* are closer to the original ballad than those from Scandinavia are not made more convincing by his emphasis on the fact that only the Scottish versions contain the artistically perfect evasions of the murderer as to the origin of the blood on his sword. These evasions certainly contribute to the tremendous artistic effect of the ballad, but emphasis on this æsthetic criterion does not help us to decide which version of the ballad is closer to the original, as Taylor's other arguments undoubtedly do. Mr M. J. C. Hodgart, in comparing the

British, French, and Scandinavian versions of *Lord Thomas and Fair Annet*[1] establishes with very great discrimination that the French version is closest to the original ballad story, but his criterion of artistic economy, which leads him to dismiss the quarrel between Eleanor and the bride as unnecessary to the story, seems to introduce subjective æsthetic considerations, and to imply that coherence and artistic success, rather than objective consistency of story-telling, are criteria of original ballad versions. Implicit artistic considerations can frequently mislead in this respect. Thus it has been said that those versions of *The Twa Sisters* or *Binnorie* in which the drowned girl's body is used to fashion the harp which proclaims her sister's crime are less original than the ones in which only her hair is used to string the harp. Now it may be admitted that the versions in which the hair is used are artistically more compelling because more economical; but, if we remember that the transformation of the whole body into the instrument of denunciation may bear witness to very primitive ideas about the magical discovery of and revenge for a hidden crime, then the less refined version, savouring so strongly of primitive magic, may be closer to the original version.

From the examples quoted it should be clear that the priority of a ballad version is not primarily a question of artistic achievement. A study of *Fause Foodrage* and of Mr Hodgart's analysis of *Lord Thomas and Fair Annet* show that the criterion of consistency of story is the safer guide, as it is unlikely that a later version brings a gain in narrative consistency for which there is no warrant in the original version.

In certain ballads there may be room for the assumption that a popular plot was tackled independently and simultaneously by various poets, and that the extant variants may not be reducible to a single original ballad, but even so it seems clear that each variant was created by an individual. The curious idea prevalent during the last century, that ballads were composed by the co-operative effort of a whole community, has little basis in what we know of creative effort in poetry, or in

[1] M. J. C. Hodgart, *The Ballads*, pp. 88 ff.

any other artistic fields, during the Middle Ages or at any other time. However responsive a community may be to artistic effort, however strongly its members may support the artist, the community as such does not create. To claim that any traditional ballad was created by a dozen men and women, however familiar with the story, who took turns in inventing stanzas or verses, and hoped that the result would be an artistically satisfactory ballad, seems grossly romantic. Why, in fact, should the origin of the traditional ballad differ materially from that of the sculptures of our cathedrals? No one would claim communal origin for the so-called Leaves of Southwell, the delightful leaf and flower ornaments in the Chapter House of Southwell Minster, or for the sculptures that adorn pre-Reformation churches in this or any other European country. Yet we do not know the names of the artists responsible for many of these, we do not know the exact date of their creation, but we do know, on the other hand, that they are the creations of individuals working in close co-operation with others, and from within a relatively small and closely knit community, whose ideas and ideals influenced the artist to a considerable extent. Why should the origin of the traditional ballad be different? Without doubt there was interaction between any community and the individual, whether a gifted amateur or itinerant minstrel, but such inter-action does not make the community as such a creative unit. Members of a community remembered the outline and often the text of a ballad, abridged or enlarged, spoiled or enhanced, and merged it with other similar ballads. The absence of written texts would account for that. In this way the gifted amateur may frequently have continued the work of the pro-fessional, and even improved on it. The artistic taste of the listener decided whether such new versions increased or decreased the value of what he heard. Only in this very restricted sense can one speak of the ballad as a communal form of art, and even in this restricted sense it might be better to speak of it as anonymous, oral, and therefore variable, rather than communal.

VII

The study of ballads, as opposed to singing or reciting them, is of comparatively recent origin, With the greater ease of printing in the later sixteenth century, and the simultaneous increase in literacy, we find printers producing single sheets—called broadsides or broadsheets, from the arrangement of the type on the paper—containing versions of traditional ballads or, more frequently, a type of poem combining certain features of traditional balladry with subject-matter not usually found there. Broadsides were the product of Elizabethan and seventeenth-century urban life, and, apart from popularizing certain aspects of literary lyrical poetry, specialized in simple narrative poetry of great immediacy and occasional charm, dealing with foreign and domestic political events, such as the troubles of the Civil War, natural phenomena, the latest floods, or the appearance of a comet, stories of fortunate and unfortunate love-affairs up and down the country, and stories of crime, usually with an edifying last speech of the criminal prior to execution. Genuine traditional ballads were frequently reproduced, sometimes, though by no means always, in versions betraying urban and literary attitudes. A case in point is *Lord Thomas and Fair Annet*, perhaps the most popular traditional ballad printed as a broadside.

Many valuable traditional ballads were preserved either intact or in forms superior to those discovered in oral circulation when students of the ballad began to listen to recitation by country folk in the nineteenth century. Oral recitation went on, and Sir Philip Sidney's blinde Crouder,[1] from whom he must have heard other ballads than *Chevy Chase*, was clearly in the oral tradition. The very considerable printing of broadsides quickly gave rise to the collection of these pieces by lovers of literature. Samuel Pepys was only one of these collectors in the course of the seventeenth century. Many other collections were made by individuals who felt that broadsides, for all their

[1] See "An Apology for Poetry," *Elizabethan Critical Essays*, edited by Gregory Smith, 1904, Vol. I, p. 178.

considerable rudeness and lack of finer literary taste, constituted popular poetry of genuine merit. Addison, in the
Spectator (Nos. 70 and 74), drew attention to the strength and
beauties of *Chevy Chase*, and devoted another essay (No. 85) to
a spirited defence of the traditional ballad, affirming that the
sentiments of *The Two Babes in the Wood* (a broadside ballad, not
a traditional ballad) "appear genuine and unaffected . . . and
are such as are the most proper to excite pity." Eighteenth-
century poets such as Ambrose Phillips, Oliver Goldsmith, and
Allan Ramsay, eager to discover unspoiled poetic instinct and
colourful incident in literature, continued the work of making
the traditional ballad acceptable to men and women of taste,
sometimes by polishing oral versions in accordance with the
more 'cultured' taste of their times.

Bishop Percy, who was perhaps stimulated to take an interest
in balladry through the mistaken notion that he was connected
with the Percy family of *Chevy Chase*, happened to come across
a dilapidated manuscript volume in the house of his friend
Humphrey Pitt of Shiffnal. This folio volume, probably collected by a famous seventeenth-century lawyer, contained
almost two hundred ballads, metrical romances, and poems,
some dating back to the fourteenth century. Like Bishop War-
burton's cook, who used pages from rare Elizabethan and
Jacobean plays for pie-covers, Pitt's servants had torn out
leaves from the Percy folio to light the fires, and two of our
most fascinating Arthurian ballads (*King Arthur and King
Cornwall* and *The Marriage of Sir Gawain*, Child, Nos. 30 and
31), were among those mutilated. But the ballads of this folio
manuscript, texts from broadsides and private songbooks, and
information from Scottish friends, such as Dalrymple, enabled
Percy to publish his famous *Reliques of Ancient English Poetry* in
1765. In the compilation of this invaluable collection Percy
did not hesitate to combine contrasting variants by smoothing
out contradictions or even to invent stanzas of his own, but
many of our most cherished ballads were given by him to the
educated public for the first time. His work contains a good
deal of poetry neither traditional in spirit nor of the ballad type,

but the influence of the genuine ballads in his *Reliques* was considerable. In fact it may be doubted whether *The Ancient Mariner* or *La Belle Dame sans Merci* would have been composed without Percy's influence. Nor can there be any doubt that when Sir Walter Scott came to read Percy as a youth the influence of the work was tremendous. "The first time," he writes, "I could scrape a few shillings together, I bought unto myself a copy of these beloved volumes; nor do I believe I ever read a book half so frequently or with half the enthusiasm." It was due to Percy's stimulus that the next important step in the appreciation and study of traditional balladry, as opposed to imitation of ballads, was reached, when Scott published in 1802 a collection of Border ballads, many of them noted down by him from the lips of singers. In *Minstrelsy of the Scottish Border* Scott preserved, on the whole, the original texts, but he was so steeped in the ballads that he occasionally joined or completed fragments, combined variants, and even invented ballads, betraying his hand in many cases by a regularity of verse technique, and by romantic attitudes at variance with the genuine versions of his great collection. His work was imitated by a number of Scottish collectors, and increasingly serious attention was given to the exact words of the ballad singers. Inspired by the methodical work of the Dane Grundtvig, who, fifty years later, began to collect every variant of Danish traditional ballads without alteration in the volumes of his monumental *Danmarks Gamle Folkeviser*, and who prefaced every ballad by a scholarly analysis of the relation of the variants and of similar ballads abroad, Francis James Child created a similar corpus of our balladry in *The English and Scottish Popular Ballads* (five folio volumes, 1882–1898). In this work every available variant of practically every extant English and Scottish ballad was gathered, each ballad prefixed by a scholarly essay on the lines of Grundtvig's collection. Relatively few new ballads were discovered in later years. There were new variants, especially those discovered by American scholars in remote communities of British stock in inaccessible parts of the U.S.A., where ballad-singing was still alive. Volumes like O. D. Campbell's and Cecil J. Sharp's *British Folk-songs from the Southern Appalachians* and Phillips Barry's *British Ballads from Maine* contain ballad versions of great beauty and interest. In these islands the collection of new variants was due, in the main, to the devoted work of Cecil J. Sharp and his friends of the Folk-song Society. The files of *The Journal of the Folk-song Society* are a mine of ballad versions, and the evidence collected in them, especially that relating to England's contribution to the stock of traditional British balladry, has not yet been fully sifted. This applies particularly to the study of ballad tunes, where British and American material is so plentiful as to require the work of a group of scholars for full evaluation.

But, while the work of ballad study goes on, the spontaneous singing of ballads has fallen a victim to rapid industrialization. Mrs Hardy, in her biography of her husband (1840–1928), significantly recounts (Vol. 1, p. 25 f.) how as a youth Hardy listened to genuine traditional ballads sung at a Dorset harvest-home. But, as she says, "It may be worthy of note that this harvest-home was among the last at which the old traditional ballads were sung, the railway having been extended to Dorchester just then, and the orally transmitted ditties of centuries being slain at a stroke by the London comic songs."

RELIGIOUS BALLADS

I

The Cherry-tree Carol

The story of this ballad-carol derives from the Apocryphal gospel of Pseudo-Matthew. Although no pre-eighteenth-century texts survive, the carol seems to go back to a much earlier period.

1. Joseph was an old man,
      and an old man was he,
   When he wedded Mary,
      in the land of Galilee.

2. Joseph and Mary walked
      through an orchard good,
   Where was cherries and berries,
      so red as any blood.

3. Joseph and Mary walked
      through an orchard green,
   Where was berries and cherries,
      as thick as might be seen.

4. O then bespoke Mary,
      so meek and so mild:
   "Pluck me one cherry, Joseph,
      for I am with child."

5. O then bespoke Joseph,
      with words most unkind:
   "Let him pluck thee a cherry
      that brought thee with child."

6. O then bespoke the babe,
   within his mother's womb;
   "Bow down then the tallest tree,
   for my mother to have some."

7. Then bowed down the highest tree
   unto his mother's hand;
   Then she cried, See, Joseph,
   I have cherries at command.

8. O then bespake Joseph:
   "I have done Mary wrong;
   But cheer up, my dearest,
   and be not cast down."

9. Then Mary plucked a cherry,
   as red as the blood,
   Then Mary went home
   with her heavy load.

10. Then Mary took her babe,
    and sat him on her knee,
    Saying, My dear son, tell me,
    what this world will be.

11. "O I shall be as dead, mother,
    as the stones in the wall;
    O the stones in the streets, mother,
    shall mourn for me all.

12. "Upon Easter-day, mother,
    my uprising shall be;
    O the sun and the moon, mother,
    shall both rise with me."

II

St Stephen and Herod

This ballad is preserved in a manuscript from about 1450. The miracle of the roasted fowl speaking seems to have originated in the East, and is preserved in the so-called *Gospel of Nicodemus*, a storehouse of medieval legend and narrative. A modern English rendering is appended.

1. Seynt Steuene was a clerk in kyng Herowdes halle,
   And seruyd him of bred and cloþ, as euery kyng befalle.

2. Steuyn out of kechone cam, wyth boris hed on honde;
   He saw a sterre was fayr and bryȝt ouer Bedlem stonde.

3. He kyst adoun þe boris hed and went in to þe halle:
   "I forsak þe, kyng Herowdes, and þi werkes alle.

4. "I forsak þe, kyng Herowdes, and þi werkes alle;
   þer is a chyld in Bedlem born is beter þan we alle."

5. "Quat eylet þe, Steuene? quat is þe befalle?
   Lakkyt þe eyþer mete or drynk in kyng Herowdes halle?"

6. "Lakit me neyþer mete ne drynk in kyng Herowdes halle;
   þer is a chyld in Bedlem born is beter þan we alle."

7. "Quat eylet þe, Steuyn? art þu wod, or þu gynnst to brede?
   Lakkyt þe eyþer gold or fe, or ony ryche wede?"

8. "Lakyt me neyþer gold ne fe, ne non ryche wede;
   þer is a chyld in Bedlem born xal helpyn vs at our nede."

9. "þat is al so soþ, Steuyn, al so soþ, iwys,
   As þis capoun crowe xal þat lyþ here in myn dysh."

10. þat word was not so sone seyd, þat word in þat halle,
þe capoun crew Cristus natus est! among þe lordes alle.

11. "Rysyt vp, myn turmentowres, be to and al be on,
And ledyt Steuyn out of þis town, and stonyt hym wyth
ston!"

12. Tokyn he Steuene, and stonyd hym in the way,
And þerfore is his euyn on Crystes owyn day.

Modern English Rendering

1. Saint Stephen was clerk in King Herod's hall
And served him with bread and cloth, as every King befalls.

2. Stephen came out of the kitchen, a boar's head in his hand,
He saw a fair and splendid star over Bethlehem stand.

3. He cast down the boar's head and went into the hall:
"I forsake thee, King Herod, and thy deeds one and all.

4. "I forsake thee, King Herod, and thy deeds one and all.
There is a child in Bethlehem born, better than us all."

5. "What ails thee, Stephen, what is it that has befallen thee?
Didst thou ever lack meat or drink in King Herod's hall?"

6. "I never lacked meat nor drink in King Herod's hall.
There is a child in Bethlehem born, better than us all."

7. "What ails thee, Stephen, are you mad or do you start to rave?
Didst thou ever lack gold or fee, or any costly weed?"

8. "I never lacked gold nor fee nor any costly weed.
There is a child in Bethlehem born that shall help us in our
need."

9. "That is as true, Stephen, as true for a certainty,
As that this capon here shall crow that's in the dish by me."

10. No sooner had that word been said, that word in that hall,
    When the capon crew, "Christ is born," among these lords all.

11. "Rise up, my tormentors, go to, all, one by one,
    Lead Stephen out of town, and stone him dead with stone."

12. Tony took Stephen and stoned him by the way,
    And therefore is his vigil on Christ's own holiday.

III

Dives and Lazarus

Dives and Lazarus were common figures of fifteenth- and sixteenth-
century moralities and interludes. The ballad concentrates medieval
religious sentiment about riches and poverty in a minimum of space.

1. As it fell out upon a day,
        Rich Dives he made a feast,
    And he invited all his friends,
        And gentry of the best.

2. Then Lazarus laid him down and down,
        And down at Dives' door:
    "Some meat, some drink, brother Dives,
        Bestow upon the poor."

3. "Thou art none of my brother, Lazarus,
        That lies begging at my door;
    No meat nor drink will I give thee,
        Nor bestow upon the poor."

4. Then Lazarus laid him down and down,
        And down at Dives' wall:
    "Some meat, some drink, brother Dives,
        Or with hunger starve I shall."

5. "Thou art none of my brother, Lazarus,
    That lies begging at my wall;
  No meat nor drink will I give thee,
    But with hunger starve you shall."

6. Then Lazarus laid him down and down,
    And down at Dives's gate:
  "Some meat, some drink, brother Dives,
    For Jesus Christ his sake."

7. "Thou art none of my brother, Lazarus,
    That lies begging at my gate;
  No meat nor drink will I give thee,
    For Jesus Christ his sake."

8. Then Dives sent out his merry men,
    To whip poor Lazarus away;
  They had no power to strike a stroke,
    But flung their whips away.

9. Then Dives sent out his hungry dogs,
    To bite him as he lay;
  They had no power to bite at all,
    But licked his sores away.

10. As it fell out upon a day,
    Poor Lazarus sickened and died;
  Then came two angels out of heaven
    His soul therein to guide.

11. "Rise up, rise up, brother Lazarus,
    And go along with me;
  For you've a place prepared in heaven,
    To sit on an angel's knee."

12. As it fell out upon a day,
    Rich Dives sickened and died;

Then came two serpents out of hell,
His soul therein to guide.

13. "Rise up, rise up, brother Dives,
And go with us to see
A dismal place, prepared in hell,
From which thou canst not flee."

14. Then Dives looked up with his eyes,
And saw poor Lazarus blest;
"Give me one drop of water, brother Lazarus,
To quench my flaming thirst.

15. "Oh had I as many years to abide
As there are blades of grass,
Then there would be an end, but now
Hell's pains will ne'er be past.

16. "Oh was I now but alive again,
The space of one half hour!
Oh that I had my peace secure!
Then the devil should have no power."

IV

Judas

This remarkable ballad is preserved in a thirteenth-century manuscript
at Trinity College, Cambridge, and is by far the oldest British ballad
extant in written form; the account of Judas's betrayal is not paralleled in
other traditional literature or related to Apocryphal sources. As in the
case of *St Stephen and Herod*, a modern English rendering is appended.

1. Hit wes upon a Scere-thorsday that ure loverd aros;
Ful milde were the wordes he spec to Judas.

2. "Judas, thou most to Jurselem, oure mete for to bugge;
Thritti platen of selver thou bere up othi rugge.

3. "Thou comest fer ithe brode stret, fer ithe brode strete;
Summe of thine tunesmen ther thou meiht imete."

4. . . . .
Imette wid is soster, the swikele wimon.

5. "Judas, thou were wrthe me stende the wid ston,
For the false prophete that tou bilevest upon."

6. "Be stille, leve soster, thin herte the tobreke!
Wiste min loverd Crist, ful wel he wolde be wreke."

7. "Judas, go thou on the roc, heie upon the ston;
Lei thin heved imy barm, slep thou the anon."

8. Sone so Judas of slepe was awake,
Thritti platen of selver from hym weren itake.

9. He drou hymselve bi the cop, that al it lavede a blode;
The Jewes out of Jurselem awenden he were wode.

10. Foret hym com the rich Jeu that heihte Pilatus:
"Wolte sulle thi loverd, that hette Jesus?"

11. "I nul sulle my loverd [for] nones cunnes eihte,
Bote hit be for the thritti platen that he me bitaihte."

12. "Wolte sulle thi Lord Crist for enes cunnes golde?"
"Nay, bote hit be for the platen that he habben wolde."

13. In him com ur Lord Crist gon, as is postles seten at mete:
"Wou sitte ye, postles, ant wi nule ye ete?"

14. "[Wou sitte ye, postles, ant wi nule ye ete?]
Ic am ibouht and isold today for oure mete."

15. Up stod him Judas: "Lord, am I that . . . ?
    "I nas never othe stude ther me the evel spec."

16. Up him stod Peter, and spec wid al his mihte,

     .   .   .   .

17. "Thau Pilatus him come wid ten hundred cnihtes,
    Yet ic wolde, loverd, for thi love fihte."

18. "Still thou be, Peter, wel I the icnowe;
    Thou wolt fursake me thrien ar the coc him crowe."

MODERN ENGLISH RENDERING

1. It was on a Maundy Thursday that our Lord rose,
   Full mild were the words that he spoke to Judas.

2. "Judas, you must go to Jerusalem to buy our meat,
   Thirty pieces of silver you must bear on your back.

3. "You will come far into the main street, far into the main street
   Some of your townsfolk you may there meet."

     .   .   .   .

4. Judas met his sister, a treacherous woman was she,

5. "Judas to be stoned to death were fit fate for thee,
   Because of the false prophet you believe in."

6. "Be still, dear sister, may your heart break in two.
   If my Lord Christ knew he would be avenged on you."

7. "Judas, come to this rock, high on this stone,
   Lay thy head in my lap and sleep anon."

8. By the time Judas from sleep did awake
   The thirty pieces of silver were taken away.

9. He beat his head that it swam with blood,
   The Jews of Jerusalem thought he was mad.

10. To him came the rich Jew, Pilate named,
    "Wilt thou sell Thy Lord, Jesus by name?"

11. "I will not sell My Lord for promised fee,
    Except for the thirty pieces he entrusted me."

12. "Wouldst thou sell thy Lord Christ for any gold?"
    "Nay, except for the [thirty] pieces that he would have."

13. Our Lord came to him as his apostles sat down for their meat:
    "How sit you, apostles, and why will you not eat?

14. "How sit you, apostles, and why will you not eat?
    I was bought and sold today for our meat."

15. Judas stood up. "Lord, am I that [wretch?]
    I never was nor stood where anyone evil spoke."

16. Peter stood up and spoke with all his might:
    .   .   .   .

17. "Though Pilate approached with a thousand knights,
    Yet I would, My Lord, for your love fight."

18. "Be still, Peter, well do I thee know,
    Thou wilt forsake me thrice before the cock crow."

BALLADS OF THE SUPERNATURAL

V

The Great Silkie of Sule Skerry

A Shetland ballad about a supernatural creature, known as a Finn, sometimes seal, sometimes man. There are Scandinavian and German ballads about unions between denizens of the sea and human beings, nearly all of them tragic. Matthew Arnold's *Forsaken Merman* is descended from these. Our ballad is perfect in its compression and in the sense of doom expressed so powerfully in the last two stanzas.

1. An eartly nourris sits and sings,
   And aye she sings, Ba, lily wean!
   Little ken I my bairnis father,
   Far less the land that he staps in.

2. Then ane arose at her bed-fit,
   An a grumly guest I'm sure was he:
   "Here am I, thy bairnis father,
   Although that I be not comelie.

3. "I am a man, upo the lan,
   An I am a silkie in the sea;
   And when I'm far and far frae lan,
   My dwelling is in Sule Skerrie."

4. "It was na weel," quo the maiden fair,
   "It was na weel, indeed," quo she,
   "That the Great Silkie of Sule Skerrie
   Suld hae come and aught a bairn to me."

5. Now he has taen a purse of goud,
   And he has pat it upo her knee,
   Sayin, Gie to me my little young son,
   An tak thee up thy nourris-fee.

6. An it sall come to pass on a simmer's day,
    When the sin shines het on evera stane,
That I will tak my little young son,
    An teach him for to swim the faem."

7. An thu sall marry a proud gunner,
    An a proud gunner I'm sure he'll be,
An the very first schot that ere he schoots,
    He'll schoot baith my young son and me.

VI

Thomas Rhymer

Thomas Erceldoune, more commonly known as Thomas Rhymer, enjoyed a great reputation as poet and seer in fourteenth-century Scotland. A person of this name appears to have lived there at that time, but it cannot be proved that the poems and prophecies attributed to him have any connexion with this elusive figure.

Like many another mythical singer, Thomas is said to have received his gifts from faery, and his story resembles that of other medieval visits to fairyland. The ballad is probably descended from an extant fifteenth-century Scottish romance about Thomas, but none of the variants can be traced back further than the eighteenth century. They do, however, preserve traditions of pre-Christian times, such as the injunction of silence, the shoes of green velvet, and, above all, the river of blood that separates faery from the natural world. The passage of Thomas through the river is an ancient symbol of rebirth, associated in many cults with the gaining of visionary insight and the beginning of a new life of religious powers.

1. True Thomas lay oer yond grassy bank,
    And he beheld a ladie gay,
A ladie that was brisk and bold,
    Come riding oer the fernie brae.

2. Her skirt was of the grass-green silk,
    Her mantel of the velvet fine,
At ilka tett of her horse's mane
    Hung fifty silver bells and nine.

3. True Thomas he took off his hat,
   And bowed him low down till his knee:
"All hail, thou mighty Queen of Heaven!
   For your peer on earth I never did see."

4. "O no, O no, True Thomas," she says,
   "That name does not belong to me;
I am but the queen of fair Elfland,
   And I'm come here for to visit thee.

*   *   *   *   *   *

5. "But ye maun go wi me now, Thomas,
   True Thomas, ye maun go wi me,
For ye maun serve me seven years,
   Thro weel or wae as may chance to be."

6. She turned about her milk-white steed,
   And took True Thomas up behind,
And aye wheneer her bridle rang,
   The steed flew swifter than the wind.

7. For forty days and forty nights
   He wade thro red blude to the knee,
And he saw neither sun nor moon,
   But heard the roaring of the sea.

8. O they rade on, and further on,
   Until they came to a garden green:
"Light down, light down, ye ladie free,
   Some of that fruit let me pull to thee."

9. "O no, O no, True Thomas," she says,
   "That fruit maun not be touched by thee,
For a' the plagues that are in hell
   Light on the fruit of this countrie.

10. "But I have a loaf here in my lap,
        Likewise a bottle of claret wine,
    And now ere we go farther on,
        We'll rest a while, and ye may dine."

11. When he had eaten and drunk his fill,
        "Lay down your head upon my knee,"
    The lady sayd, "ere we climb yon hill,
        And I will show you fairlies three.

12. "O see not ye yon narrow road,
        So thick beset wi thorns and briers?
    That is the path of righteousness,
        Tho after it but few enquires.

13. "And see not ye that braid braid road,
        That lies across yon lillie leven?
    That is the path of wickedness,
        Tho some call it the road to heaven.

14. "And see not ye that bonny road,
        Which winds about the fernie brae?
    That is the road to fair Elfland,
        Whe[re] you and I this night maun gae.

15. "But Thomas, ye maun hold your tongue,
        Whatever you may hear or see,
    For gin ae word you should chance to speak,
        You will neer get back to your ain countrie."

16. He has gotten a coat of the even cloth,
        And a pair of shoes of velvet green,
    And till seven years were past and gone
        True Thomas on earth was never seen.

VII

King Orfeo

In spite of difficulties of dialect this ballad repays study. There exists a much longer minstrel poem of the fourteenth century on the same subject, resembling our ballad in that Orfeo wins back his Lady Heurodis from the King of Faery by the power of his song. The minstrel poem and our ballad are adaptations of the Greek myth of Orpheus and Eurydice, in which the singer, Orpheus, unsuccessfully tries to lead his dead wife back from the Underworld. As a result of medieval and especially Celtic tradition, the barren Underworld of the Greek myth has become the Land of Faery, the Lady is not really dead but enchanted, and everything ends happily.

The original reciter of our ballad had forgotten a number of stanzas after stanzas four and eight, the first omission relating, as he remembered, the carrying away of the lady by fairies, and the King's pursuit, until one day he saw her as a member of a company of fairies passing him and entering a castle in a hillside. (In the minstrel poem the Land of Faery is reached by a long passage through a rock, which finally leads Orfeo to a green and level country of eternal summer.) The second omission, after stanza eight, related that a messenger invited Orfeo to the Castle of Faery to entertain the company with his playing.

The refrain of the ballad is corrupt Scandinavian, not surprising in view of its Shetland origin. The two lines probably mean:

> Early green's the wood
> Where the hart goes yearly.

1. Der lived a king inta da aste,
    Scowan ürla grün
   Der lived a lady in da wast.
    Whar giorten han grün oarlac

2. Dis king he has a huntin gaen,
   He's left his Lady Isabel alane.

3. "Oh I wis ye'd never gaen away,
   For at your hame is döl an wae.

4. "For da king o Ferrie we his daert,
    Has pierced your lady to da hert."

*   *   *   *   *

5. And aifter dem da king has gaen,
    But whan he cam it was a grey stane.

6. Dan he took oot his pipes ta play,
    Bit sair his hert wi döl an wae.

7. And first he played da notes o noy,
    An dan he played da notes o joy.

8. An dan he played da göd gabber reel,
    Dat meicht ha made a sick hert hale.

*   *   *   *   *

9. "Noo come ye in inta wir ha,
    An come ye in among wis a'."

10. Now he's gaen in inta der ha,
    An he's gaen in among dem a'.

11. Dan he took out his pipes to play,
    Bit sair his hert wi döl an wae.

12. An first he played da notes o noy,
    An dan he played da notes o joy

13. An dan he played da göd gabber reel,
    Dat meicht ha made a sick hert hale.

14. "Noo tell to us what ye will hae:
    What sall we gie you for your play?"

15. "What I will hae I will you tell,
    An dat's me Lady Isabel"

16. "Yees tak your lady, an yees gaeng hame,
    An yees be king ower a' your ain."

17. He's taen his lady, and he's gaen hame,
    An noo he's king ower a' his ain.

VIII

Tam Lin

This dramatic ballad, unsurpassed of its kind, appears to be of considerable age. *The Tayl of the Yong Tamlene*, and a dance, *Thom of Lyn*, are listed in the anonymous *Complaynt of Scotland* (1549) to which attention has been drawn (p. 42), while *A Ballett of Thomalyn* is found as an entry in the Stationers' Register for 1558. It has been suggested that Burns is responsible for the lovely stanzas thirty-six and thirty-seven.

The central incident of this ballad—the disenchantment of the hero by the heroine, and the assumption of various shapes in this process—is found in a Cretan fairy-tale, recorded during the last century, which in turn goes back to pre-Homeric traditions of the marriage of Peleus, the father of Achilles, to Thetis. In both Greek instances the woman is the disenchanted shape-shifter, otherwise the resemblance to *Tam Lin* is surprisingly close. It must remain a moot point whether this emphasis on transmigration goes back to beliefs common to many Indo-European peoples or whether the idea of transmigration was borrowed from the written literature of other nations. The problem is discussed by A. H. Krappe in *Science of Folk-lore*.[1]

1. O I forbid you, maidens a',
       That wear gowd on your hair,
   To come or gae by Carterhaugh,
       For young Tam Lin is there.

2. There's nane that gaes by Carterhaugh
       But they leave him a wad,

[1] Methuen, 1930.

Either their rings, or green mantles,
   Or else their maidenhead.

3. Janet has kilted her green kirtle
   A little aboon her knee,
And she has broded her yellow hair
   A little aboon her bree,
And she's awa to Carterhaugh,
   As fast as she can hie.

4. When she came to Carterhaugh
   Tam Lin was at the well,
And there she fand his steed standing,
   But away was himsel.

5. She had na pu'd a double rose,
   A rose but only twa,
Till up then started young Tam Lin,
   Says, Lady, thou's pu nae mae.

6. Why pu's thou the rose, Janet,
   And why breaks thou the wand?
Or why comes thou to Carterhaugh
   Withoutten my command?

7. "Carterhaugh, it is my ain,
   My daddie gave it me;
I'll come and gang by Carterhaugh,
   And ask nae leave at thee."

      *   *   *   *   *

8. Janet has kilted her green kirtle
   A little aboon her knee,
And she has snooded her yellow hair
   A little aboon her bree,
And she is to her father's ha,
   As fast as she can hie.

9. Four and twenty ladies fair
   Were playing at the ba,
   And out then cam the fair Janet,
   Ance the flower amang them a'.

10. Four and twenty ladies fair
    Were playing at the chess,
    And out then cam the fair Janet,
    As green as onie glass.

11. Out then spak an auld grey knight,
    Lay oer the castle wa,
    And says, Alas, fair Janet, for thee
    But we'll be blamed a'.

12. "Haud your tongue, ye auld fac'd knight,
    Some ill death may ye die!
    Father my bairn on whom I will,
    I'll father nane on thee."

13. Out then spak her father dear,
    And he spak meek and mild;
    "And ever alas, sweet Janet," he says,
    "I think thou gaes wi child."

14. "If that I gae wi child, father,
    Mysel maun bear the blame;
    There's neer a laird aboot your ha
    Shall get the bairn's name.

15. "If my love were an earthly knight,
    As he's an elfin grey,
    I wad na gie my ain true-love
    For nae lord that ye hae.

16. "The steed that my true-love rides on
    Is lighter than the wind;

Wi siller he is shod before,
  Wi burning gowd behind."

17. Janet has kilted her green kirtle
      A little aboon her knee,
    And she has snooded her yellow hair
      A little aboon her bree,
    And she's awa to Carterhaugh,
      As fast as she can hie.

18. When she cam to Carterhaugh,
      Tam Lin was at the well,
    And there she fand his steed standing,
      But away was himsel.

19. She had na pu'd a double rose,
      A rose but only twa,
    Till up then started young Tam Lin,
      Says, Lady, thou pu's nae mae.

20. Why pu's thou the rose, Janet,
      Amang the groves sae green,
    And a' to kill the bonie babe
      That we gat us between?

21. "O tell me, tell me, Tam Lin," she says,
      "For's sake that died on tree,
    If eer ye was in holy chapel,
      Or christendom did see?"

22. "Roxbrugh he was my grandfather,
      Took me with him to bide,
    And ance it fell upon a day
      That wae did me betide.

23. "And ance it fell upon a day,
      A cauld day and a snell,

When we were frae the hunting come,
    That frae my horse I fell;
The Queen o Fairies she caught me,
    In yon green hill to dwell.

24. "And pleasant is the fairy land,
    But, an eerie tale to tell,
Ay at the end of seven years
    We pay a tiend to hell;
I am sae fair and fu o flesh,
    I'm feard it be mysel.

25. "But the night is Halloween, lady,
    The morn is Hallowday;
Then win me, win me, an ye will,
    For weel I wat ye may.

26. "Just at the mirk and midnight hour
    The fairy folk will ride,
And they that wad their true-love win,
    At Miles Cross they maun bide."

27. "But how shall I thee ken, Tam Lin,
    Or how my true-love know,
Amang sae mony unco knights
    The like I never saw?"

28. "O first let pass the black, lady,
    And syne let pass the brown,
But quickly run to the milk-white steed,
    Pu ye his rider down.

29. "For I'll ride on the milk-white steed,
    And ay nearest the town;
Because I was an earthly knight
    They gie me that renown.

30. "My right hand will be glovd, lady,
       My left hand will be bare,
   Cockt up shall my bonnet be,
       And kaimd down shall my hair,
   And thae's the takens I gie thee,
       Nae doubt I will be there.

31. "They'll turn me in your arms, lady,
       Into an esk and adder;
   But hold me fast, and fear me not,
       I am your bairn's father.

32. "They'll turn me to a bear sae grim,
       And then a lion bold;
   But hold me fast, and fear me not,
       As ye shall love your child.

33. "Again they'll turn me in your arms
       To a red het gaud of airn;
   But hold me fast, and fear me not
       I'll do to you nae harm.

34. "And last they'll turn me in your arms
       Into the burning gleed;
   Then throw me into well water,
       O throw me in wi speed.

35. "And then I'll be your ain true-love,
       I'll turn a naked knight;
   Then cover me wi your green mantle,
       And cover me out o sight."

36. Gloomy, gloomy was the night,
       And eerie was the way,
   As fair Jenny in her green mantle
       To Miles Cross she did gae.

37. About the middle o the night
       She heard the bridles ring;
    This lady was as glad at that
       As any earthly thing.

38. First she let the black pass by,
       And syne she let the brown;
    But quickly she ran to the milk-white steed,
       And pu'd the rider down.

39. Sae weel she minded what he did say,
       And young Tam Lin did win;
    Syne coverd him wi her green mantle,
       As blythe's a bird in spring.

40. Out then spak the Queen o Fairies,
       Out of a bush o broom:
    "Them that has gotten young Tam Lin
       Has gotten a stately groom."

41. Out then spak the Queen o Fairies,
       And an angry woman was she:
    "Shame betide her ill-far'd face,
       And an ill death may she die,
    For she's taen awa the boniest knight
       In a' my companie.

42. "But had I kend, Tam Lin," she says,
       "What now this night I see,
    I wad hae taen out thy twa grey een,
       And put in twa een o tree."

IX

Allison Gross

An attractive ballad, unique in that it shows two supernatural powers, the maleficent witch and the beneficent Queen of Faery, at odds.

Stanza twelve is of great interest for the student of folk-lore: the "seely ['silly,' in the sense of 'happy'] court" is the fairy rout, familiar from *Tam Lin* and from many a folk-tale; the gowan, or daisy, enjoyed a cult of its own during the Middle Ages, and was associated with the beneficent aspects of supernatural powers; "Hallow-even" (the night of October 31 to November 1) is the favourite time for mortals to see the fairy folk riding—it was originally the Celtic New Year, and on that day the fairy mounds stood open so that communication between mortals and immortals was possible. That the Queen of Faery should step on to a bank of daisies in the depths of autumn may seem inappropriate, but fairy folk are the spirits of vegetation, green like the grass and the leaves they personify, and wherever they go there is eternal summer.

1. O Allison Gross, that lives in yon towr,
   The ugliest witch i the north country,
   Has trysted me ae day up till her bowr,
   An monny fair speech she made to me.

2. She stroaked my head, an she kembed my hair,
   An she set me down saftly on her knee;
   Says, Gin ye will be my lemman so true,
   Sae monny braw things as I would you gi.

3. She showd me a mantle o red scarlet,
   Wi gouden flowrs an fringes fine;
   Says, Gin ye will be my lemman so true,
   This goodly gift it sal be thine.

4. "Awa, awa, ye ugly witch,
   Haud far awa, an lat me be;
   I never will be your lemman sae true,
   An I wish I were out o your company."

5. She neist brought a sark o the saftest silk,
   Well wrought wi pearles about the ban;
   Says, Gin you will be my ain true love,
   This goodly gift you sal comman.

6. She showd me a cup of the good red gold,
   Well set wi jewls sae fair to see;
   Says, Gin you will be my lemman sae true,
   This goodly gift I will you gi.

7. "Awa, awa, ye ugly witch,
   Had far awa, and lat me be;
   For I woudna ance kiss your ugly mouth
   For a' the gifts that ye coud gi."

8. She's turnd her right and roun about,
   An thrice she blaw on a grass-green horn,
   An she sware by the meen and the stars abeen,
   That she'd gar me rue the day I was born.

9. Then out has she taen a silver wand,
   An she's turnd her three times roun an roun;
   She's mutterd sich words till my strength it faild,
   An I fell down senceless upon the groun.

10. She's turnd me into an ugly worm,
    And gard me toddle about the tree;
    An ay, on ilka Saturdays night,
    My sister Maisry came to me,

11. Wi silver bason an silver kemb,
    To kemb my heady upon her knee;
    But or I had kissd her ugly mouth,
    I'd rather a toddled about the tree.

12. But as it fell out on last Hallow-even,
    When the seely court was ridin by,

The queen lighted down on a gowany bank,
　Nae far frae the tree where I wont to lye.

13. She took me up in her milk-white han,
　　An she's stroakd me three times oer her knee;
　She chang'd me again to my ain proper shape,
　　An I nae mair maun toddle about the tree.

X

Clark Colven

The Great Silkie of Sule Skerry was about a union between a merman
and an earthly woman; traditional ballads of many countries tell of the
loves of earthly men and mermaidens, and in nearly all cases the earthly
lover comes to a tragic end, frequently because of his inconstancy—like
Clark Colven (or Clerk Colvill) of our ballad—sometimes because of his
unwillingness to enter upon such a union. The German *Knight of Staufen-
berg* belongs to this group of stories, which is seen to perfection in the
Danish ballad of *Sir Oluf*. The Breton ballad *Seigneur Nann* suggests
Celtic connexions, and has spread over all France.

The title *Clark Colven* has been chosen as being more familiar than
Clerk Colvill.

1. Clark Colven and his gay ladie,
　　As they walked to yon garden green,
　A belt about her middle gimp,
　　Which cost Clark Colven crowns fifteen:

2. "O hearken weel now, my good lord,
　　O hearken weel to what I say;
　When ye gang to the wall o Stream,
　　O gang nae neer the well-fared may."

3. "O haud your tongue, my gay ladie,
　　Tak nae sic care o me;
　For I nae saw a fair woman
　　I like so well as thee."

4. He mounted on his berry-brown steed,
       And merry, merry rade he on,
   Till he came to the wall o Stream,
       And there he saw the mermaiden.

5. "Ye wash, ye wash, ye bonny may,
       And ay's ye wash your sark o silk:"
   "It's a' for you, ye gentle knight,
       My skin is whiter than the milk."

6. He's taen her by the milk-white hand,
       He's taen her by the sleeve sae green,
   And he's forgotten his gay ladie,
       And away with the fair maiden.

       *   *   *   *   *   *

7. "Ohon, alas!" says Clark Colven,
       "And aye sae sair's I mean my head!"
   And merrily leugh the mermaiden,
       "O win on till you be dead.

8. "But out ye tak your little pen-knife,
       And frae my sark ye shear a gare;
   Row that about your lovely head,
       And the pain ye'll never feel nae mair."

9. Out he has taen his little pen-knife,
       And frae her sark he's shorn a gare,
   Rowed that about his lovely head,
       But the pain increased mair and mair.

10. "Ohon, alas!" says Clark Colven,
       "An aye sae sair's I mean my head!"
    And merrily laughd the mermaiden,
       "It will ay be war till ye be dead."

11. Then out he drew his trusty blade,
    And thought wi it to be her dead,
But she's become a fish again,
    And merrily sprang into the fleed.

12. He's mounted on his berry-brown steed,
    And dowy, dowy rade he home,
And heavily, heavily lighted down
    When to his ladie's bower-door he came.

13. "Oh, mither, mither, mak my bed,
    And, gentle ladie, lay me down;
Oh, brither, brither, unbend my bow,
    'T will never be bent by me again."

14. His mither she has made his bed,
    His gentle ladie laid him down,
His brither he has unbent his bow,
    'T was never bent by him again.

XI

The Unquiet Grave

That undue mourning disturbs the rest of the departed is a widespread belief, both Christian and pre-Christian. It supplies the principal plot for the next three ballads. The ballad of *The Unquiet Grave*, which has few rivals for lyrical poignancy of sorrow in ballad poetry, or indeed in all poetry, expresses the underlying emotions perfectly. There are many variants, all with beauties of their own. Professor Gerould has noted the opening couplet of eight variants to show how impossible it is to select any one as the original, as all are equally evocative. Two versions of the opening stanza which may be compared with the variant selected run:

Cold blows the wind oer my true love,
    Cold blow the drops of rain;
I never, never had but one sweetheart,
    In the greenwood he was slain.

and:

> O wet and weary is the night
> And evedown pours the rain,
> And he that was sae true to me
> Lies in the greenwood slain.

It will be noticed that, compared with our full version, in these variants the sex of dead and mourner are exchanged, not a matter of great importance, but interesting in comparing the English ballad to the lovely Danish ballad on a related subject, *The Betrothed in the Grave*. A deeply moving epic treatment of the motif of excessive mourning may be found in the Eddic lay of *Helgi, the Slayer of Hunding*, which also influenced the ballad of *Earl Brand*.

1.   "The wind doth blow today, my love,
      And a few small drops of rain;
  I never had but one true-love,
      In cold grave she was lain.

2.   "I'll do as much for my true-love
      As any young man may;
  I'll sit and mourn all at her grave
      For a twelvemonth and a day."

3.   The twelvemonth and a day being up,
      The dead began to speak:
  "Oh who sits weeping on my grave,
      And will not let me sleep?"

4.   "'Tis I, my love, sits on your grave,
      And will not let you sleep;
  For I crave one kiss of your clay-cold lips,
      And that is all I seek."

5.   "You crave one kiss of my clay-cold lips;
      But my breath smells earthy strong;
  If you have one kiss of my clay-cold lips,
      Your time will not be long.

6.   "'T is down in yonder garden green,
      Love, where we used to walk,

The finest flower that ere was seen
Is withered to a stalk.

7. "The stalk is withered dry, my love,
So will our hearts decay;
So make yourself content, my love,
Till God calls you away."

XII

Sweet William's Ghost

Another ballad about a lover's ghost returning to his pining sweetheart. The Danish ballad referred to in the introductory note to the previous ballad is perhaps superior to our ballad. The variant chosen was recorded by the Scottish poet Allan Ramsay before 1740.

1. There came a ghost to Margret's door,
With many a grievous groan,
And ay he tirled at the pin,
But answer made she none.

2. "Is that my father Philip,
Or is 't my brother John?
Or is 't my true-love, Willy,
From Scotland new come home?"

3. "'T is not thy father Philip,
Nor yet thy brother John;
But 't is thy true-love, Willy,
From Scotland new come home.

4. "O sweet Margret, O dear Margret,
I pray thee speak to me;
Give me my faith and troth, Margret,
As I gave it to thee."

5. "Thy faith and troth thou's never get,
   Nor yet will I thee lend,
   Till that thou come within my bower,
   And kiss my cheek and chin."

6. "If I shoud come within thy bower,
   I am no earthly man;
   And shoud I kiss thy rosy lips,
   Thy days will not be lang.

7. "O sweet Margret, O dear Margret,
   I pray thee speak to me;
   Give me my faith and troth, Margret,
   As I gave it to thee."

8. "Thy faith and troth thou's never get,
   Nor yet will I thee lend,
   Till you take me to yon kirk,
   And wed me with a ring."

9. "My bones are buried in yon kirk-yard,
   Afar beyond the sea,
   And it is but my spirit, Margret,
   That's now speaking to thee."

10. She stretchd out her lilly-white hand,
    And, for to do her best,
    "Hae, there's your faith and troth, Willy,
    God send your soul good rest."

11. Now she has kilted her robes of green
    A piece below her knee,
    And a' the live-lang winter night
    The dead corp followed she.

12. "Is there any room at your head, Willy?
    Or any room at your feet?

Or any room at your side, Willy,
    Wherein that I may creep?"

13. "There's no room at my head, Margret,
    There's no room at my feet;
There's no room at my side, Margret,
    My coffin's made so meet."

14. Then up and crew the red, red cock,
    And up then crew the gray:
"Tis time, tis time, my dear Margret,
    That you were going away."

15. No more the ghost to Margret said,
    But, with a grievous groan,
Evanishd in a cloud of mist,
    And left her all alone.

16. "O stay, my only true-love, stay,"
    The constant Margret cry'd;
Wan grew her cheeks, she closd her een,
    Stretchd her soft limbs, and dy'd.

XIII

The Wife of Usher's Well

This ballad has been discussed in the Introduction. Birch was associated with the dead and with rebirth in popular superstition.

1. There lived a wife at Usher's Well,
    And a wealthy wife was she;
She had three stout and stalwart sons,
    And sent them oer the sea.

2. They hadna been a week from her,
　　A week but barely ane,
　Whan word came to the carline wife
　　That her three sons were gane.

3. They hadna been a week from her,
　　A week but barely three,
　Whan word came to the carlin wife
　　That her sons she'd never see.

4. "I wish the wind may never cease,
　　Nor fashes in the flood,
　Till my three sons come hame to me,
　　In earthly flesh and blood."

5. It fell about the Martinmass,
　　When nights are lang and mirk,
　The carlin wife's three sons came hame,
　　And their hats were o the birk.

6. It neither grew in syke nor ditch,
　　Nor yet in ony sheugh;
　But at the gates o Paradise,
　　That birk grew fair eneugh.

　　　*　　*　　*　　*　　*　　*

7. "Blow up the fire, my maidens,
　　Bring water from the well;
　For a' my house shall feast this night,
　　Since my three sons are well."

8. And she has made to them a bed,
　　She's made it large and wide,
　And she's taen her mantle her about,
　　Sat down at the bed-side.

　　　*　　*　　*　　*　　*　　*

9. Up then crew the red, red cock,
   And up and crew the gray;
   The eldest to the youngest said,
   'T is time we were away.

10. The cock he hadna crawd but once,
    And clappd his wings at a',
    When the youngest to the eldest said,
    Brother, we must awa.

11. "The cock doth craw, the day doth daw,
    The channerin worm doth chide;
    Gin we be mist out o our place,
    A sair pain we maun bide.

12. "Fare ye weel, my mother dear!
    Fareweel to barn and byre!
    And fare ye weel, the bonny lass
    That kindles my mother's fire!

XIV

Lady Isabel and the Elf-knight

Some of the problems of this extraordinarily widespread ballad have
been discussed in the Introduction. There are innumerable North
American versions, apart from those from the Continent. Probably an
Italian short story of the late fourteenth century should be stressed as the
most important single source of this ballad group.

Thomas Hardy heard a Dorset version (sometimes known as *May
Colven*) on the occasion of a harvest-home in the 1850's.

1. Fair lady Isabel sits in her bower sewing,
      Aye as the gowans grow gay
   There she heard an elf-knight blawing his horn.
      The first morning in May

2. "If I had yon horn that I hear blawing,
   And yon elf-knight to sleep in my bosom."

3. This maiden had scarcely these words spoken,
   Till in at her window the elf-knight has luppen.

4. "It's a very strange matter, fair maiden," said he,
   "I canna blaw my horn but ye call on me.

5. "But will ye go to yon greenwood side?
   If ye canna gang, I will cause you to ride."

6. He leapt on a horse, and she on another,
   And they rode on to the greenwood together.

7. "Light down, light down, lady Isabel," said he,
   "We are come to the place where ye are to die."

8. "Hae mercy, hae mercy, kind sir, on me,
   Till ance my dear father and mother I see."

9. "Seven king's-daughters here hae I slain,
   And ye shall be the eight o them."

10. "O sit down a while, lay your head on my knee,
    That we may hae some rest before that I die."

11. She stroakd him sae fast, the nearer he did creep,
    Wi a sma charm she lulld him fast asleep.

12. Wi his ain sword-belt sae fast as she ban him,
    Wi his ain dag-durk sae sair as she dang him.

13. "If seven king's-daughters here ye hae slain,
    Lye ye here, a husband to them a'."

TRAGIC BALLADS

XV

The Twa Sisters (*Binnorie*)

Something has been said in the Introduction (pp. 33, 55) about this fine ballad, sometimes known as *Binnorie* from the supposed place of the crime. This ballad, of which there are many Scandinavian versions, was first printed in 1656.

Binnorie should be accented on the second syllable.

1. There were two sisters, they went playing,
   With a hie downe downe a downe-a

   To see their father's ships come sayling in.
   With a hy downe downe a downe-a

2. And when they came unto the sea-brym,
   The elder did push the younger in.

3. "O sister, O sister, take me by the gowne,
   And drawe me up upon the dry ground."

4. "O sister, O sister, that may not bee,
   Till salt and oatmeale grow both of a tree."

5. Somtymes she sanke, somtymes she swam,
   Until she came unto the mill-dam.

6. The miller runne hastily downe the cliffe,
   And up he betook her withouten her life.

7. What did he doe with her brest-bone?
   He made him a violl to play thereupon.

8. What did he doe with her fingers so small?
   He made him peggs to his violl withall.

9. What did he doe with her nose-ridge?
   Unto his violl he made him a bridge.

10. What did he doe with her veynes so blew?
    He made him strings to his violl thereto.

11. What did he doe with her eyes so bright?
    Upon his violl he played at first sight.

12. What did he doe with her tongue so rough?
    Unto the violl it spake enough.

13. What did he doe with her two shinnes?
    Unto the violl they danc'd Moll Syms.

14. Then bespake the treble string,
    "O yonder is my father the king."

15. Then bespake the second string,
    "O yonder sitts my mother the queen."

16. And then bespake the strings all three,
    "O yonder is my sister that drowned mee."

17. "Now pay the miller for his payne,
    And let him bee gone in the divel's name."

XVI

Lord Randal

Enough has been said in the Introduction (pp. 38, 39) to show the interesting problems connected with this ballad. The strictness of the dialogue-form with its repetition and mounting suspense suggests very conscious artistic effort. The ballad was immensely popular in the United States.

A

1. "O where ha you been, Lord Randal, my son?
   And where ha you been, my handsome young man?"
   "I ha been at the greenwood; mother, mak my bed
       soon,
   For I'm wearied wi hunting, and fain wad lie down."

2. "An wha met ye there, Lord Randal, my son?
   And wha met you there, my handsome young man?"
   "O I met wi my true-love; mother, mak my bed soon,
   For I'm wearied wi huntin, an fain wad lie down."

3. "And what did she give you, Lord Randal, my son?
   And what did she give you, my handsome young man?"
   "Eels fried in a pan; mother, mak my bed soon,
   For I'm wearied wi huntin, and fain wad lie down."

4. "And wha gat your leavins, Lord Randal, my son?
   And wha gat your leavins, my handsom young man?"
   "My hawks and my hounds; mother, mak my bed
       soon,
   For I'm wearied wi hunting, and fain wad lie down."

5. "And what becam of them, Lord Randal, my son?
   And what becam of them, my handsome young man?"
   "They stretched their legs out an died; mother, mak
       my bed soon,
   For I'm wearied wi huntin, and fain wad lie down."

6. "O I fear you are poisoned, Lord Randal, my son!
   I fear you are poisoned, my handsome young man!"
   "O yes, I am poisoned; mother, mak my bed soon,
   For I'm sick at the heart, and I fain wad lie down."

7. "What d'ye leave to your mother, Lord Randal, my son?
   What d'ye leave to your mother, my handsome young
      man?"
   "Four and twenty milk kye; mother, mak my bed soon,
   For I'm sick at the heart, and I fain wad lie down."

8. "What d'ye leave to your sister, Lord Randal, my son?
   What d'ye leave to your sister, my handsome young
      man?"
   "My gold and my silver; mother, mak my bed soon,
   For I'm sick at the heart, and I fain wad lie down."

9. "What d'ye leave to your brother, Lord Randal, my son?
   What d'ye leave to your brother, my handsome young
      man?"
   "My houses and my lands; mother, mak my bed soon,
   For I'm sick at the heart, and I fain wad lie down."

10. "What d'ye leave to your true-love, Lord Randal, my
       son?
    What d'ye leave to your true-love, my handsome young
       man?"
    "I leave her hell and fire; mother, mak my bed soon,
    For I'm sick at the heart, and I fain wad lie down."

B

1. "O whare hae ye been a' day, Lord Donald, my son?
   O whare hae ye been a' day, my jollie young man?"
   "I've been awa courtin; mither, mak my bed sune,
   For I'm sick at the heart, and I fain wad lie doun."

2. "What wad ye hae for your supper, Lord Donald, my
   son?
   What wad ye hae for your supper, my jollie young
   man?"
   "I've gotten my supper; mither, mak my bed sune,
   For I'm sick at the heart, and I fain wad lie doun."

3. "What did ye get to your supper, Lord Donald, my
   son?
   What did ye get to your supper, my jollie young man?"
   "A dish of sma fishes; mither, mak my bed sune,
   For I'm sick at the heart, and I fain wad lie doun."

4. "Whare gat ye the fishes, Lord Donald, my son?
   Whare gat ye the fishes, my jollie young man?"
   "In my father's black ditches; mither, mak my bed
   sune,
   For I'm sick at the heart, and I fain wad lie doun."

5. "What like were your fishes, Lord Donald, my son?
   What like were your fishes, my jollie young man?"
   "Black backs and spreckld bellies; mither, mak my
   bed sune,
   For I'm sick at the heart, and I fain wad lie doun."

6. "O I fear ye are poisond, Lord Donald, my son!
   O I fear ye are poisond, my jollie young man!"
   "O yes! I am poisond; mither, mak my bed sune,
   For I'm sick at the heart, and I fain wad lie doun."

7. "What will ye leave to your father, Lord Donald, my
   son?
   What will ye leave to your father, my jollie young
   man?"
   "Baith my houses and land; mither, mak my bed
   sune,
   For I'm sick at the heart, and I fain wad lie doun."

8. "What will ye leave to your brither, Lord Donald, my
     son?
   What will ye leave to your brither, my jollie young
     man?"
   "My horse and the saddle; mither, mak my bed sune,
   For I'm sick at the heart, and I fain wad lie doun."

9. "What will ye leave to your sister, Lord Donald, my
     son?
   What will ye leave to your sister, my jollie young
     man?"
   "Baith my gold box and rings; mither, mak my bed
     sune,
   For I'm sick at the heart, and I fain wad lie doun."

10. "What will ye leave to your true-love, Lord Donald,
      my son?
    What will ye leave to your true-love, my jollie young
      man?"
    "The tow and the halter, for to hang on yon tree,
    And lat her hang there for the poysoning o me."

XVII

Edward

This noble ballad has exact counterparts in Denmark, Sweden, and
Finland. It was given to Bishop Percy by Sir David Dalrymple, who, in
turn, probably had it from an author with literary pretensions, who
employed consciously archaic language. On the other hand, it is a perfectly legitimate development of genuine ballad tradition.

1. "Why dois your brand sae drap wi bluid,
                                    Edward, Edward,
   Why dois your brand sae drap wi bluid,
       And why sae sad gang yee O?"

"O I hae killed my hauke sae guid,
                    Mither, mither,
O I hae killed my hauke sae guid,
    And I had nae mair bot hee O."

2. "Your haukis bluid was nevir sae reid,
                    Edward, Edward,
Your haukis bluid was nevir sae reid,
    My deir son I tell thee O."
"O I hae killed my reid-roan steid,
                    Mither, mither,
O I hae killed my reid-roan steid,
    That erst was sae fair and frie O."

3. "Your steid was auld, and ye hae gat mair,
                    Edward, Edward,
Your steid was auld, and ye hae gat mair,
    Sum other dule ye drie O."
"O I hae killed my fadir deir,
                    Mither, mither,
O I hae killed my fadir deir,
    Alas, and wae is mee O!"

4. "And whatten penance wul ye drie for that,
                    Edward, Edward?
And whatten penance will ye drie for that?
    My deir son, now tell me O."
"Ile set my feit in yonder boat,
                    Mither, mither,
Ile set my feit in yonder boat,
    And Ile fare ovir the sea O."

5. "And what wul ye doe wi your towirs and your ha,
                    Edward, Edward?
And what wul ye doe wi your towirs and your ha,
    That were sae fair to see O?"

"Ile let thame stand tul they doun fa,
                    Mither, mither,
Ile let thame stand tul they doun fa,
    For here nevir mair maun I bee O."

6. "And what wul ye leive to your bairns and your wife,
                    Edward, Edward?
And what wul ye leive to your bairns and your wife,
    Whan ye gang ovir the sea O?"
"The warldis room, late them beg thrae life,
                    Mither, mither,
The warldis room, late them beg thrae life,
    For thame nevir mair wul I see O."

7. "And what wul ye leive to your ain mither deir,
                    Edward, Edward?
And what wul ye leive to your ain mither deir?
    My deir son, now tell me O."
"The curse of hell frae me sall ye beir,
                    Mither, mither,
The curse of hell frae me sall ye beir,
    Sic counseils ye gave to me O."

XVIII

The Twa Brothers

Variants of six early nineteenth-century Scottish versions have been
discovered in the United States in recent years.

1. There were twa brethren in the north,
    They went to school thegither;
   The one unto the other said,
    Will you try a warsle afore?

2. They warsled up, they warsled down,
    Till Sir John fell to the ground,

And there was a knife in Sir Willie's pouch,
    Gied him a deadlie wound.

3. "Oh brither dear, take me on your back,
    Carry me to yon burn clear,
And wash the blood from off my wound,
    And it will bleed nae mair."

4. He took him up upon his back,
    Carried him to yon burn clear,
And washd the blood from off his wound,
    But aye it bled the mair.

5. "Oh brither dear, take me on your back,
    Carry me to yon kirk-yard,
And dig a grave baith wide and deep,
    And lay my body there."

6. He's taen him up upon his back,
    Carried him to yon kirk-yard,
And dug a grave baith deep and wide,
    And laid his body there.

7. "But what will I say to my father dear,
    Gin he chance to say, Willie, whar's John?"
"Oh say that he's to England gone,
    To buy him a cask of wine."

8. "And what shall I say to my mother dear,
    Gin she chance to say, Willie, whar's John?"
"Oh say that he's to England gone,
    To buy her a new silk gown."

9. "And what will I say to my sister dear,
    Gin she chance to say, Willie, whar's John?"
"O say that he's to England gone,
    To buy her a wedding ring."

10. "What will I say to her you loe dear,
      Gin she cry, Why tarries my John?"
    "Oh tell her I lie in Kirk-land fair,
      And home again will never come."

XIX

The Three Ravens

The ballad of *The Three Ravens*, first printed in 1611, seems to have enjoyed great popularity well into the nineteenth century. The transformation of the sweetheart into a doe may go back to very early beliefs in shape-shifting, and adds a curiously eerie touch. It is interesting to note that in an American version the ballad has a happy ending, the ravens directing the knight's friends, who bear the man to a hut and feed and tend him.

1. There were three rauens sat on a tree,
       Downe a downe, hay down, hay downe
   There were three rauens sat on a tree,
       With a downe
   There were three rauens sat on a tree,
   They were as blacke as they might be.
       With a downe derrie, derrie, derrie, downe,
       downe

2. The one of them said to his mate,
   "Where shall we our breakefast take?"

3. "Downe in yonder greene field,
   There lies a knight slain vnder his shield.

4. "His hounds they lie downe at his feete,
   So well they can their master keepe.

5. "His haukes they flie so eagerly,
   There's no fowle dare him come nie."

6. Downe there comes a fallow doe,
   As great with yong as she might goe.

7. She lift vp his bloudy hed,
   And kist his wounds that were so red.

8. She got him vp vpon her backe,
   And carried him to earthen lake.

9. She buried him before the prime,
   She was dead herselfe ere euen-song time.

10. God send euery gentleman,
   Such haukes, such hounds, and such a leman.

XX

Bewick and Graham

"Bully" here means a sworn brother. Old Grahame's grief at his son's
lack of letters reminds one of Chaucer's Franklin.

1. Old Grahame [he] is to Carlisle gone,
   Where Sir Robert Bewick there met he;
 In arms to the wine they are gone,
   And drank till they were both merry.

2. Old Grahame he took up the cup,
   And said, "Brother Bewick, here's to thee;
 And here's to our two sons at home,
   For they live best in our country."

3. "Nay, were thy son as good as mine,
   And of some books he could but read,
 With sword and buckler by his side,
   To see how he could save his head,

4. "They might have been calld two bold brethren
      Where ever they did go or ride;
   They might [have] been calld two bold brethren,
      They might have crackd the Borderside.

5. "Thy son is bad, and is but a lad,
      And bully to my son cannot be;
   For my son Bewick can both write and read,
      And sure I am that cannot he."

6. "I put him to school, but he would not learn,
      I bought him books, but he would not read;
   But my blessing he's never have
      Till I see how his hand can save his head."

7. Old Grahame called for an account,
      And he askd what was for to pay;
   There he paid a crown, so it went round,
      Which was all for good wine and hay.

8. Old Grahame is into the stable gone,
      Where stood thirty good steeds and three;
   He's taken his own steed by the head,
      And home rode he right wantonly.

9. When he came home, there did he espy,
      A loving sight to spy or see,
   There did he espy his own three sons,
      Young Christy Grahame, the foremost was he.

10. There did he espy his own three sons,
      Young Christy Grahame, the foremost was he:
   "Where have you been all day, father,
      That no counsel you would take by me?"

11. "Nay, I have been in Carlisle town,
      Where Sir Robert Bewick there met me;

He said thou was bad, and calld thee a lad,
    And a baffled man by thou I be.

12. "He said thou was bad, and calld thee a lad,
    And bully to his son cannot be;
For his son Bewick can both write and read,
    And sure I am that cannot thee.

13. "I put thee to school, but thou would not learn,
    I bought thee books, but thou would not read;
But my blessing thou's never have
    Till I see with Bewick thou can save thy head."

14. "Oh, pray forbear, my father dear;
    That ever such a thing should be!
Shall I venture my body in field to fight
    With a man that's faith and troth to me?"

15. "What's that thou sayst, thou limmer loon?
    Or how dare thou stand to speak to me?
If thou do not end this quarrel soon,
    Here is my glove thou shalt fight me."

16. Christy stoopd low unto the ground,
    Unto the ground, as you'll understand:
"O father, put on your glove again,
    The wind hath blown it from your hand."

17. "What's that thou sayst, thou limmer loon?
    Or how dare thou stand to speak to me?
If thou do not end this quarrel soon,
    Here is my hand thou shalt fight me."

18. Christy Grahame is to his chamber gone,
    And for to study, as well might be,
Whether to fight with his father dear,
    Or with his bully Bewick he.

19. "If it be [my] fortune my bully to kill,
     As you shall boldly understand,
   In every town that I ride through,
     They'll say, There rides a brotherless man!

20. "Nay, for to kill my bully dear,
     I think it will be a deadly sin;
   And for to kill my father dear,
     The blessing of heaven I neer shall win.

21. "O give me your blessing, father," he said,
     "And pray well for me for to thrive;
   If it be my fortune my bully to kill,
     I swear I'll neer come home alive."

22. He put on his back a good plate-jack,
     And on his head a cap of steel,
   With sword and buckler by his side;
     O gin he did not become them well!

23. "O fare thee well, my father dear!
     And fare thee well, thou Carlisle town!
   If it be my fortune my bully to kill,
     I swear I'll neer eat bread again."

24. Now we'll leave talking of Christy Grahame,
     And talk of him again belive;
   But we will talk of bonny Bewick,
     Where he was teaching his scholars five.

25. Now when he had learnd them well to fence,
     To handle their swords without any doubt,
   He's taken his own sword under his arm,
     And walkd his father's close about.

26. He lookd between him and the sun,
     To see what farleys he coud see;

There he spy'd a man with armour on,
  As he came riding over the lee.

27. "I wonder much what man yon be
      That so boldly this way does come;
    I think it is my nighest friend,
      I think it is my bully Grahame.

28. "O welcome, O welcome, bully Grahame!
      O man, thou art my dear, welcome!
    O man, thou art my dear, welcome!
      For I love thee best in Christendom."

29. "Away, away, O bully Bewick,
      And of thy bullyship let me be!
    The day is come I never thought on;
      Bully, I'm come here to fight with thee."

30. "O no! not so, O bully Grahame!
      That eer such a word should spoken be!
    I was thy master, thou was my scholar:
      So well as I have learnëd thee."

31. "My father he was in Carlisle town,
      Where thy father Bewick there met he;
    He said I was bad, and he calld me a lad,
      And a baffled man by thou I be."

32. "Away, away, O bully Grahame,
      And of all that talk, man, let us be!
    We'll take three men of either side
      To see if we can our fathers agree."

33. "Away, away, O bully Bewick,
      And of thy bullyship let me be!
    But if thou be a man, as I trow thou art,
      Come over this ditch and fight with me."

34. "O no! not so, my bully Grahame!
      That eer such a word should spoken be!
    Shall I venture my body in field to fight
      With a man that's faith and troth to me?"

35. "Away, away, O bully Bewick,
      And of all that care, man, let us be!
    If thou be a man, as I trow thou art,
      Come over this ditch and fight with me."

36. "Now, if it be my fortune thee, Grahame, to kill,
      As God's will's, man, it all must be;
    But if it be my fortune thee, Grahame, to kill,
      'T is home again I'll never gae."

37. "Thou art of my mind then, bully Bewick,
      And sworn-brethren will we be;
    If thou be a man, as I trow thou art,
      Come over this ditch and fight with me."

38. He flang his cloak from [off] his shoulders,
      His psalm-book out of his hand flang he,
    He clapd his hand upon the hedge,
      And oer lap he right wantonly.

39. When Grahame did see his bully come,
      The salt tear stood long in his eye:
    "Now needs must I say that thou art a man,
      That dare venture thy body to fight with me.

40. "Now I have a harness on my back;
      I know that thou hath none on thine;
    But as little as thou hath on thy back,
      Sure as little shall there be on mine."

41. He flang his jack from off his back,
      His steel cap from his head flang he;

He's taken his sword into his hand,
    He's tyed his horse unto a tree.

42. Now they fell to it with two broa[d swords],
    For two long hours fought Bewick [and he];
Much sweat was to be seen on them both,
    But never a drop of blood to see.

43. Now Grahame gave Bewick an ackward stroke,
    An ackward stroke surely struck he;
He struck him now under the left breast,
    Then down to the ground as dead fell he.

44. "Arise, arise, O bully Bewick,
    Arise, and speak three words to me!
Whether this be thy deadly wound,
    Or God and good surgeons will mend thee."

45. "O horse, O horse, O bully Grahame,
    And pray do get thee far from me!
Thy sword is sharp, it hath wounded my heart,
    And so no further can I gae.

46. "O horse, O horse, O bully Grahame,
    And get thee far from me with speed!
And get thee out of this country quite!
    That none may know who's done the deed."

47. "O if this be true, my bully dear,
    The words that thou dost tell to me,
The vow I made, and the vow I'll keep;
    I swear I'll be the first that die."

48. Then he stuck his sword in a moody-hill,
    Where he lap thirty good foot and three;
First he bequeathed his soul to God,
    And upon his own sword-point lap he.

49. Now Grahame he was the first that died,
      And then came Robin Bewick to see;
   "Arise, arise, O son!" he said,
      "For I see thou's won the victory.

50. "Arise, arise, O son!" he said,
      "For I see thou's won the victory:"
   "[Father, co]uld ye not drunk your wine at home,
      [And le]tten me and my brother be?

51. "Nay, dig a grave both low and wide,
      And in it us two pray bury;
   But bury my bully Grahame on the sunside,
      For I'm sure he's won the victory."

52. Now we'll leave talking of these two brethren,
      In Carlisle town where they lie slain,
   And talk of these two good old men,
      Where they were making a pitiful moan.

53. With that bespoke now Robin Bewick:
      "O man, was I not much to blame?
   I have lost one of the liveliest lads
      That ever was bred unto my name."

54. With that bespoke my good lord Grahame:
      "O man, I have lost the better block;
   I have lost my comfort and my joy,
      I have lost my key, I have lost my lock.

55. "Had I gone through all Ladderdale,
      And forty horse had set on me,
   Had Christy Grahame been at my back,
      So well as he woud guarded me."

56. I have no more of my song to sing,
      But two or three words to you I'll name;
   But 't will be talk'd in Carlisle town
      That these two [old] men were all the blame.

BALLADS OF LOVE

XXI

Earl Brand

This ballad has been fully discussed in the Introduction. One variant, known as *The Douglas Tragedy*, was collected and probably thoroughly rewritten by Scott.

1. Did ye ever hear o guid Earl o Bran
   An the queen's daughter o the south-lan?

2. She was na fifteen years o age
   Till she came to the Earl's bed-side.

3. "O guid Earl o Bran, I fain wad see
   My grey hounds run over the lea."

4. "O kind lady, I have no steeds but one,
   But ye shall ride, an I shall run."

5. "O guid Earl o Bran, but I have tua,
   An ye shall hae yere wael o those."

6. The're ovr moss an the're over muir,
   An they saw neither rich nor poor.

7. Till they came to ald Carl Hood,
   He's ay for ill, but he's never for good.

8. "O guid Earl o Bran, if ye loe me,
   Kill Carl Hood an gar him die."

9. "O kind lady, we had better spare;
   I never killd ane that wore grey hair.

10. "We'll gie him a penny-fie an let him gae,
    An then he'll carry nae tiddings away."

11. "Where hae been riding this lang simmer-day?
    Or where hae stolen this lady away?"

12. "O I hae not riden this lang simmer-day,
    Nor hae I stolen this lady away.

13. "For she is my sick sister
    I got at the Wamshester."

14. "If she were sick an like to die,
    She wad na be wearing the gold sae high."

15. Ald Carl Hood is over the know,
    Where they rode one mile, he ran four.

16. Till he came to her mother's yetts,
    An I wat he rapped rudely at.

17. "Where is the lady o this ha?"
    "She's out wie her maidens, playing at the ba."

18. "O na! fy na!
    For I met her fifteen miles awa.

19. "She's over moss, an she's over muir,
    An a' to be the Earl o Bran's whore."

20. Some rode wie sticks, an some wie rungs,
    An a' to get the Earl o Bran slain.

21. That lady lookd over her left shoudder-bane:
    "O guid Earl o Bran, we'll a' be taen!
    For yond'r a' my father's men.

22. "But if ye'll take my claiths, I'll take thine,
    An I'll fight a' my father's men."

23. "It's no the custom in our land
    For ladies to fight an knights to stand.

24. "If they come on me ane by ane,
    I'll smash them a' doun bane by bane.

25. "If they come on me ane and a',
    Ye soon will see my body fa."

26. He has luppen from his steed,
    An he has gein her that to had.

27. An bad her never change her cheer
    Untill she saw his body bleed.

28. They came on him ane by ane,
    An he smashed them doun a' bane by bane.

29. He sat him doun on the green grass,
    For I wat a wearit man he was.

30. But ald Carl Hood came him behind,
    An I wat he gae him a deadly wound.

31. He's awa to his lady then,
    He kissed her, and set her on her steed again.

32. He rode whistlin out the way.
    An a' to hearten his lady gay.

33. 'Till he came to the water-flood:
    "O guid Earl o Bran, I see blood!"

34. "O it is but my scarlet hood,
    That shines upon the water-flood."

35. They came on 'till his mother's yett,
    An I wat he rappit poorly at.

36. His mother she's come to the door:
    "O son, ye've gotten yere dead wie an English
          whore!"

37. "She was never a whore to me;
    Sae let my brother her husband be."

38. Sae ald Carl Hood was not the dead o ane,
    But he was the dead o hale seeventeen.

XXII

Clerk Saunders

There are Scandinavian versions of this ballad, adaptations of which
seem to have enjoyed great popularity in Scotland. As in the previous
ballad, the rival claims of kin and love are at work to produce tragedy.

1. Clerk Saunders and a gay lady
       Was walking in yonder green,
   And heavy, heavy was the love
       That fell this twa lovers between.

2. "A bed, a bed," Clerk Saunders said,
       "And ay a bed for you and me;"
   "Never a ane," said the gay lady,
       "Till ance we twa married be.

3. "There would come a' my seven brethern,
       And a' their torches burning bright,
   And say, We hae but ae sister,
       And behad, she's lying wi you the night."

4. "You'll take a napkain in your hand,
      And then you will tie up your een;
   Then you may swear, and safe your aith,
      You sawna Sandy sin yestreen.

5. "You'll take me up upo your back,
      And then you'll carry me to your bed;
   Then you may swear, and save your aith,
      Your board[-floor] Sandy never tred."

6. She's taen him upo her back,
      And she's carried him unto her bed,
   That she might swear, and safe her aith,
      Her board-floor Sandy never tread.

7. She's taen a napkin in her hand,
      And lo she did tie up her een,
   That she might swear, and safe her aith,
      She sawna Sandy syne yestreen.

8. They were na weel into the room,
      Nor yet laid weel into the bed,

         .   .   .   .   .

            .   .   .   .   .

9. When in came a' her seven brethern,
      And a' their torches burning bright;
   Says they, We hae but ae sister,
      And behold, she's lying wi you this night.

10. "I," bespake the first o them,
      A wat an ill death mat he die!
    "I bear a brand into my hand
      Shall quickly gar Clerk Saunders die."

11. "I," bespake the second of them,
      A wat a good death mat he die!

"We will gae back, let him alane,
   His father has nae mair but he."

12. "I," bespake the third o them,
   A wat an ill death mat he die!
"I bear the brand into my hand
   Shall quickly help to gar him die."

13. "I," bespake the fourth o them,
   A wat a good death mat he die!
"I bear the brand into my hand
   Shall never help to gar him die."

14. "I," bespake the fifth o them,
   A wat an ill death mat he die!
"Altho his father hae nae mair,
   I'll quickly help to gar him die."

15. "I," bespake the sixth o them,
   A wat a good death mat he die!
"He's a worthy earl's son,
   I'll never help to gar him die."

16. "I," bespake the seventh of them,
   A wat an ill death mat he die!
"I bear the brand into my hand
   Shall quickly gar Clerk Saunders die."

17. They baith lay still, and sleeped sound,
   Untill the sun began to sheen;
She drew the curtains a wee bit,
   And dull and drowsie was his een.

18. "This night," said she, "the sleepiest man
   That ever my twa eyes did see
Hay lyen by me, and sweat the sheets;
   A wite they're a great shame to see."

19. She rowd the claiths a' to the foot,
    And then she spied his deadly wounds:
    "O wae be to my seven brethern,
    A wat an ill death mat they die!

20. "I'm sure it was neither rogue nor loun
    I had into my bed wi me;
    'T was Clerk Saunders, that good earl's son,
    That pledgd his faith to marry me."

XXIII

Sheath and Knife

The ballad poet's treatment of a theme that might easily lead to sensationalism is magnificently restrained. Stanza nine is one of the supreme achievements of ballad poetry: it has an imaginative certainty worthy of Shakespeare and Wordsworth.

1. One king's daughter said to anither,
       Brume blumes bonnie and grows sae fair
   "We'll gae ride like sister and brither."
       And we'll neer gae down to the brume nae mair

2. "We'll ride doun into yonder valley,
   Whare the greene green trees are budding sae gaily.

3. "Wi hawke and hounde we will hunt sae rarely,
   And we'll come back in the morning early."

4. They rade on like sister and brither,
   And they hunted and hawket in the valley thegether.

5. "Now, lady, hauld my horse and my hawk,
   For I maun na ride, and I downa walk.

6. "But set me doun be the rute o this tree,
    For there hae I dreamt that my bed sall be."

7. The ae king's dochter did lift doun the ither,
    And she was licht in her armis like ony fether.

8. Bonnie Lady Ann sat doun be the tree,
    And a wide grave was houkit whare nane suld be.

9. The hawk had nae lure, and the horse had nae master,
    And the faithless hounds thro the woods ran faster.

10. The one king's dochter has ridden awa,
    But bonnie Lady Ann lay in the deed-thraw.

XXIV

Lord Thomas and Fair Annet

Lord Thomas and Fair Annet has enjoyed tremendous popularity in this country and in the U.S.A., and was printed again and again as a broadside. In this way the text of the ballad was stabilized. The Percy version printed here is almost certainly the rehandling of a traditional version by a fine poet, as is shown by the consciously archaic language.

The rose and the briar, growing from the tombs of the dead lovers, are found in many other British and Continental ballads, and go back to the immortal tale of Tristan and Iseult and its sources.

1. Lord Thomas and Fair Annet
    Sate a' day on a hill;
    Whan night was cum, and sun was sett,
    They had not talkt their fill.

2. Lord Thomas said a word in jest,
    Fair Annet took it ill:
    "A, I will nevir wed a wife
    Against my ain friends' will."

3. "Gif ye wull nevir wed a wife,
    A wife wull neir wed yee:"
Sae he is hame to tell his mither,
    And knelt upon his knee.

4. "O rede, O rede, mither," he says,
    "A gude rede gie to mee;
O sall I tak the nut-browne bride,
    And let Faire Annet bee?"

5. "The nut-browne bride haes gowd and gear,
    Fair Annet she has gat nane;
And the little beauty Fair Annet haes
    O it wull soon be gane."

6. And he has till his brother gane:
    "Now, brother, rede ye mee;
A, sall I marrie the nut-browne bride,
    And let Fair Annet bee?"

7. "The nut-browne bride has oxen, brother,
    The nut-browne bride has kye;
I wad hae ye marrie the nut-browne bride,
    And cast Fair Annet bye."

8. "Her oxen may dye i the house, billie,
    And her kye into the byre,
And I sall hae nothing to mysell
    Bot a fat fadge by the fyre."

9. And he has till his sister gane:
    "Now, sister, rede ye mee;
O sall I marrie the nut-browne bride,
    And set Fair Annet free?"

10. "I'se rede ye tak Fair Annet, Thomas,
    And let the browne bride alane;

Lest ye sould sigh, and say, Alace,
    What is this we brought hame!"

11. "No, I will tak my mither's counsel,
    And marrie me owt o hand;
    And I will tak the nut-browne bride,
    Fair Annet may leive the land."

12. Up then rose Fair Annet's father,
    Twa hours or it wer day,
    And he is gane into the bower
    Wherein Fair Annet lay.

13. "Rise up, rise up, Fair Annet," he says,
    "Put on your silken sheene;
    Let us gae to St Marie's kirke,
    And see that rich weddeen."

14. "My maides, gae to my dressing-roome,
    And dress to me my hair;
    Whaireir yee laid a plait before,
    See yee lay ten times mair.

15. "My maids, gae to my dressing-room,
    And dress to me my smock;
    The one half is o the holland fine,
    The other o needle-work."

16. The horse Fair Annet rade upon,
    He amblit like the wind;
    Wi siller he was shod before,
    Wi burning gowd behind.

17. Four and twanty siller bells
    Wer a' tyed till his mane,
    And yae tift o the norland wind,
    They tinkled ane by ane.

18. Four and twenty gay gude knichts
    Rade by Fair Annet's side,
And four and twenty fair ladies.
    As gin she had bin a bride.

19. And whan she cam to Marie's kirk,
    She sat on Marie's stean:
The cleading that Fair Annet had on
    It skinkled in their een.

20. And whan she cam into the kirk,
    She shimmerd like the sun;
The belt that was about her waist
    Was a' wi pearles bedone.

21. She sat her by the nut-browne bride,
    And her een they were sae clear,
Lord Thomas he clean forgat the bride,
    Whan Fair Annet drew near.

22. He had a rose into his hand,
    He gae it kisses three,
And reaching by the nut-browne bride,
    Laid it on Fair Annet's knee.

23. Up than spak the nut-browne bride,
    She spak wi meikle spite:
"And whair gat ye that rose-water,
    That does mak yee sae white?"

24. "O I did get the rose-water
    Whair ye wull neir get nane,
For I did get that very rose-water
    Into my mither's wame."

25. The bride she drew a long bodkin
    Frae out her gay head-gear,

And strake Fair Annet unto the heart,
     That word spak nevir mair.

26. Lord Thomas he saw Fair Annet wex pale,
     And marvelit what mote bee;
   But whan he saw her dear heart's blude,
     A' wood-wroth wexed hee.

27. He drew his dagger, that was sae sharp,
     That was sae sharp and meet,
   And drave it into the nut-browne bride,
     That fell deid at his feit.

28. "Now stay for me, dear Annet," he sed,
     "Now stay, my dear," he cry'd;
   Then strake the dagger untill his heart,
     And fell deid by her side.

29. Lord Thomas was buried without kirk-wa,
     Fair Annet within the quiere,
   And o the tane thair grew a birk,
     The other a bonny briere.

30. And ay they grew, and ay they threw,
     As they wad faine be neare;
   And by this ye may ken right weil
     They were twa luvers deare.

XXV

Little Musgrave and Lady Barnard

This is one of our greatest tragic ballads. Every incident seems to be brought to life with the greatest imaginative economy. A very great number of American versions have been collected, some of them preserving a setting almost a hundred years older than that in the oldest British versions.

1. As it fell one holy-day,
        Hay downe
     As many be in the yeare,
   When young men and maids together did goe,
     Their mattins and masse to heare,

2. Little Musgrave came to the church-dore;
     The preist was at private masse;
   But he had more minde of the faire women
     Then he had of our lady['s] grace.

3. The one of them was clad in green,
     Another was clad in pall,
   And then came in my lord Bernard's wife,
     The fairest amonst them all.

4. She cast an eye on Little Musgrave,
     As bright as the summer sun;
   And then bethought this Little Musgrave,
     This lady's heart have I woonn.

5. Quoth she, I have loved thee, Little Musgrave,
     Full long and many a day;
   "So have I loved you, fair lady,
     Yet never word durst I say."

6. "I have a bower at Buckelsfordbery,
      Full daintyly it is deight;
   If thou wilt wend thither, thou Little Musgrave,
      Thou's lig in mine armes all night."

7. Quoth he, I thank yee, faire lady,
      This kindnes thou showest to me;
   But whether it be to my weal or woe,
      This night I will lig with thee.

8. With that he heard, a little tynë page,
      By his ladye's coach as he ran:
   "All though I am my ladye's foot-page,
      Yet I am Lord Barnard's man.

9. "My lord Barnard shall knowe of this,
      Whether I sink or swim;"
   And ever where the bridges were broake
      He laid him downe to swimme.

10. "A sleepe or wake, thou Lord Barnard,
      As thou art a man of life,
   For Little Musgrave is at Bucklesfordbery,
      A bed with thy own wedded wife."

11. "If this be true, thou little tinny page,
      This thing thou tellest to me,
   Then all the land in Bucklesfordbery
      I freely will give to thee.

12. "But if it be a ly, thou little tinny page,
      This thing thou tellest to me,
   On the hyest tree in Bucklesfordbery
      Then hanged shalt thou be."

13. He called up his merry men all:
      "Come saddle me my steed;

This night must I to Buckellsfordbery,
  For I never had greater need."

14. And some of them whistld, and some of them sung,
      And some these words did say,
    And ever when my lord Barnard's horn blew,
      "Away, Musgrave, away!"

15. "Methinks I hear the thresel-cock,
      Methinks I hear the jaye;
    Methinks I hear my lord Barnard,
      And I would I were away."

16. "Lye still, lye still, thou Little Musgrave,
      And huggell me from the cold;
    'T is nothing but a shephard's boy,
      A driving his sheep to the fold.

17. "Is not thy hawke upon a perch?
      Thy steed eats oats and hay;
    And thou a fair lady in thine armes,
      And wouldst thou bee away?"

18. With that my lord Barnard came to the dore,
      And lit a stone upon;
    He plucked out three silver keys,
      And he opend the dores each one.

19. He lifted up the coverlett,
      He lifted up the sheet;
    "How now, how now, thou Littell Musgrave,
      Doest thou find my lady sweet?"

20. "I find her sweet," quoth Little Musgrave,
      "The more 't is to my paine;
    I would gladly give three hundred pounds
      That I were on yonder plaine."

21. "Arise, arise, thou Littell Musgrave,
        And put thy clothës on;
     It shall nere be said in my country
        I have killed a naked man.

22. "I have two swords in one scabberd,
        Full deere they cost my purse;
     And thou shalt have the best of them,
        And I will have the worse."

23. The first stroke that Little Musgrave stroke,
        He hurt Lord Barnard sore;
     The next stroke that Lord Barnard stroke,
        Little Musgrave nere struck more.

24. With that bespake this faire lady,
        In bed whereas she lay;
     "Although thou'rt dead, thou Little Musgrave,
        Yet I for thee will pray.

25. "And wish well to thy soule will I,
        So long as I have life;
     So will I not for thee, Barnard,
        Although I am thy wedded wife."

26. He cut her paps from off her brest;
        Great pitty it was to see
     That some drops of this ladie's heart's blood
        Ran trickling downe her knee.

27. "Woe worth you, woe worth, my mery men all,
        You were nere borne for my good;
     Why did you not offer to stay my hand,
        When you see me wax so wood?

28. "For I have slaine the bravest sir knight
        That ever rode on steed;

So have I done the fairest lady
That ever did woman's deed.

29. "A grave, a grave," Lord Barnard cryd,
"To put these lovers in;
But lay my lady on the upper hand,
For she came of the better kin."

XXVI

Bonny Barbara Allen

Oliver Goldsmith said: "The music of the finest singer is dissonance to what I felt when our old dairy-maid sung me into tears with *Johnny Armstrong's Last Goodnight* or *The Cruelty of Barbara Allen*." (*Essays*, 1765, p. 14.)

1. It was in and about the Martinmas time,
When the green leaves were a falling,
That Sir John Græme, in the West Country,
Fell in love with Barbara Allan.

2. He sent his man down through the town,
To the place where she was dwelling:
"O haste and come to my master dear,
Gin ye be Barbara Allan."

3. O hooly, hooly rose she up,
To the place where he was lying,
And when she drew the curtain by,
"Young man, I think you're dying."

4. "O it's I'm sick, and very, very sick,
And 't is a' for Barbara Allan:"
"O the better for me ye's never be,
Tho your heart's blood were a spilling.

5. "O dinna ye mind, young man," said she,
    "When ye was in the tavern a drinking,
   That ye made the healths gae round and round,
    And slighted Barbara Allan?"

6. He turnd his face unto the wall,
    And death was with him dealing:
   "Adieu, adieu, my dear friends all,
    And be kind to Barbara Allan."

7. And slowly, slowly raise she up,
    And slowly, slowly left him,
   And sighing said, she coud not stay,
    Since death of life had reft him.

8. She had not gane a mile but twa,
    When she heard the dead-bell ringing,
   And every jow that the dead-bell geid,
    It cry'd, Woe to Barbara Allan!

9. "O mother, mother, make my bed!
    O make it saft and narrow!
   Since my love died for me to-day,
    I'll die for him to-morrow."

XXVII

The Braes o Yarrow

The selected variant of this moving ballad of bitter feud and tragic love
is in the handwriting of James Hogg, the Ettrick shepherd, and preserved
among Scott's material for *Minstrelsy of the Scottish Border*. There is
another version, equally moving, in Percy.

1. Late at een, drinkin the wine,
    Or early in a mornin,
   The set a combat them between,
    To fight it in the dawnin.

2. "O stay at hame, my noble lord!
    O stay at hame, my marrow!
My cruel brother will you betray,
    On the dowy houms o Yarrow."

3. "O fare ye weel, my lady gaye!
    O fare ye weel, my Sarah!
For I maun gae, tho I neer return
    Frae the dowy banks o Yarrow."

4. She kissd his cheek, she kaimd his hair,
    As she had done before, O;
She belted on his noble brand,
    An he's awa to Yarrow.

5. O he's gane up yon high, high hill—
    I wat he gaed wi sorrow—
An in a den spied nine armd men,
    I the dowy houms o Yarrow.

6. "O ir ye come to drink the wine,
    As ye hae doon before, O?
Or ir ye come to wield the brand,
    On the bonny banks o Yarrow?"

7. "I im no come to drink the wine,
    As I hae don before, O,
But I im come to wield the brand,
    On the dowy houms o Yarrow."

8. Four he hurt, an five he slew,
    On the dowy houms o Yarrow,
Till that stubborn knight came him behind,
    An ran his body thorrow.

9. "Gae hame, gae hame, good-brother John,
    An tell your sister Sarah

To come an lift her noble lord,
    Who's sleepin sound on Yarrow."

10. "Yestreen I dreamd a dolefu dream;
    I kend there wad be sorrow;
    I dreamd I pu'd the heather green,
    On the dowy banks o Yarrow."

11. She gaed up yon high, high hill—
    I wat she gaed wi sorrow—
    An in a den spy'd nine dead men,
    On the dowy houms o Yarrow.

12. She kissd his cheek, she kaimd his hair,
    As oft she did before, O;
    She drank the red blood frae him ran,
    On the dowy houms o Yarrow.

13. "O haud your tongue, my douchter dear,
    For what needs a' this sorrow?
    I'll wed you on a better lord
    Than him you lost on Yarrow."

14. "O haud your tongue, my father dear,
    An dinna grieve your Sarah;
    A better lord was never born
    Than him I lost on Yarrow.

15. "Tak hame your ousen, tak hame your kye,
    For they hae bred our sorrow;
    I wiss that they had a' gane mad
    Whan they cam first to Yarrow."

XXVIII

Rare Willie drowned in Yarrow, or *The Water o Gamrie*

This simple and moving ballad was recorded first in 1733.

1. "Willy's rare, and Willy's fair,
      And Willy's wondrous bony,
   And Willy heght to marry me,
      Gin eer he marryd ony.

2. "Yestreen I made my bed fu brade,
      The night I'll make it narrow,
   For a' the live-long winter's night
      I lie twin'd of my marrow.

3. "O came you by yon water-side?
      Pu'd you the rose or lilly?
   Or came you by yon meadow green?
      Or saw you my sweet Willy?"

4. She sought him east, she sought him west,
      She sought him brade and narrow;
   Sine, in the clifting of a craig,
      She found him drownd in Yarrow.

XXIX and XXX

Young Beichan and *Hind Horn*

About a hundred years after the death of Thomas à Becket a story not unlike that of this popular ballad was told of his father. But the helpful Saracen maiden, the wedding of the faithless groom interrupted in the nick of time, and the happy ending are commonplaces of medieval romance.

The ballad of *Hind Horn*, whose story is told in three Middle English verse romances, tells essentially the same tale with the sexes reversed, and romances and ballads of the German hero, Henry the Lion, contain the very same incident as *Hind Horn*.

Young Beichan

1. In London city was Bicham born,
      He longd strange countries for to see,
   But he was taen by a savage Moor,
      Who handld him right cruely.

2. For thro his shoulder he put a bore,
      An thro the bore has pitten a tree,
   An he's gard him draw the carts o wine,
      Where horse and oxen had wont to be.

3. He's casten [him] in a dungeon deep,
      Where he coud neither hear nor see;
   He's shut him up in a prison strong,
      An he's handld him right cruely.

4. O this Moor he had but ae daughter,
      I wot her name was Shusy Pye;
   She's doen her to the prison-house,
      And she's calld Young Bicham one word by.

5. "O hae ye ony lands or rents,
      Or citys in your ain country,

      Coud free you out of prison strong,
        An coud mantain a lady free?"

6. "O London city is my own,
      An other citys twa or three,
    Coud loose me out o prison strong
      An coud mantain a lady free.

7. O she has bribed her father's men
      Wi meikle goud and white money,
    She's gotten the key o the prison doors,
      An she has set Young Bicham free.

8. She's gi'n him a loaf o good white bread,
      But an a flask o Spanish wine,
    An she bad him mind on the ladie's love
      That sae kindly freed him out o pine.

9. "Go set your foot on good ship-board,
      An haste you back to your ain country,
    An before that seven years has an end,
      Come back again, love, and marry me."

10. It was long or seven years had an end
      She longd fu sair her love to see;
    She's set her foot on good ship-board,
      An turned her back on her ain country.

11. She's saild up, so has she doun,
      Till she came to the other side;
    She's landed at Young Bicham's gates,
      An I hop this day she sal be his bride.

12. "Is this Young Bicham's gates?" says she,
      "Or is that noble prince within?"
    "He's up the stairs wi his bonny bride,
      An monny a lord and lady wi him."

13. "O has he taen a bonny bride,
       An has he clean forgotten me!"
    An sighing said that gay lady,
       I wish I were in my ain country!

14. But she's pitten her han in her pocket,
       An gin the porter guineas three;
    Says, Take ye that, ye proud porter,
       An bid the bridegroom speak to me.

15. O whan the porter came up the stair,
       He's fa'n low down upon his knee:
    "Won up, won up, ye proud porter,
       An what makes a' this courtesy?"

16. "O I've been porter at your gates
       This mair nor seven years an three,
    But there is a lady at them now
       The like of whom I never did see.

17. "For on every finger she has a ring,
       An on the mid-finger she has three,
    An there's as meikle goud aboon her brow
       As woud buy an earldome o lan to me."

18. Then up it started Young Bicham,
       An sware so loud by Our Lady,
    "It can be nane but Shusy Pye,
       That has come oer the sea to me."

19. O quickly ran he down the stair,
       O fifteen steps he has made but three;
    He's tane his bonny love in his arms,
       An a wot he kissd her tenderly.

20. "O hae you tane a bonny bride?
       An hae you quite forsaken me?

An hae ye quite forgotten her
That gae you life an liberty?"

21. She's lookit oer her left shoulder
    To hide the tears stood in her ee;
    "Now fare thee well, Young Bicham," she says,
    "I'll strive to think nae mair on thee."

22. "Take back your daughter, madam," he says,
    "An a double dowry I'll gi her wi;
    For I maun marry my first true love,
    That's done and suffered so much for me."

23. He's take his bonny love by the han,
    And led her to yon fountain stane;
    He's changd her name frae Shusy Pye,
    An he's cald her his bonny love, Lady Jane.

Hind Horn

1. In Scotland there was a babie born,
    Lill lal, etc.
  And his name it was called young Hind Horn,
    With a fal lal, etc.

2. He sent a letter to our king
    That he was in love with his daughter Jean.

3. He's gien to her a silver wand,
    With seven living lavrocks sitting thereon.

4. She's gien to him a diamond ring,
    With seven bright diamonds set therein.

5. "When this ring grows pale and wan,
    You may know by it my love is gane."

6. One day as he looked his ring upon,
   He saw the diamonds pale and wan.

7. He left the sea and came to land,
   And the first that he met was an old beggar man.

8. "What news, what news?" said young Hind Horn;
   "No news, no news," said the old beggar man.

9. "No news," said the beggar, "no news at a',
   But there is a wedding in the king's ha.

10. "But there is a wedding in the king's ha,
    That has halden these forty days and twa."

11. "Will ye lend me your begging coat?
    And I'll lend you my scarlet cloak.

12. "Will you lend me your beggar's rung?
    And I'll gie you my steed to ride upon.

13. "Will you lend me your wig o hair,
    To cover mine, because it is fair?"

14. The auld beggar man was bound for the mill,
    But young Hind Horn for the king's hall

15. The auld beggar man was bound for to ride,
    But young Hind Horn was bound for the bride.

16. When he came to the king's gate,
    He sought a drink for Hind Horn's sake.

17. The bride came down with a glass of wine,
    When he drank out the glass, and dropt in the ring.

18. "O got ye this by sea or land?
    Or got ye it off a dead man's hand?"

19. "I got not it by sea, I got it by land,
And I got it, madam, out of your own hand."

20. "O I'll cast off my gowns of brown,
And beg wi you frae town to town.

21. "O I'll cast off my gowns of red,
And I'll beg wi you to win my bread."

22. "Ye needna cast off your gowns of brown,
For I'll make you lady o many a town.

23. "Ye needna cast off your gowns of red,
It's only a sham, the begging o my bread."

24. The bridegroom he had wedded the bride,
But young Hind Horn he took her to bed.

XXXI

The Maid freed from the Gallows

Enough has been said in the Introduction (pp. 37, 38) about this simple ballad to show its wide dissemination and appeal. It is related to a widespread folk-tale in which the girl is threatened with punishment for having lost a golden ball.

1. "O good Lord Judge, and sweet Lord Judge,
Peace for a little while!
Methinks I see my own father,
Come riding by the stile.

2. "Oh father, oh father, a little of your gold,
And likewise of your fee!
To keep my body from yonder grave,
And my neck from the gallows-tree."

3. "None of my gold now you shall have,
        Nor likewise of my fee:
    For I am come to see you hangd,
        And hanged you shall be."

4. "Oh good Lord Judge, and sweet Lord Judge,
        Peace for a little while!
    Methinks I see my own mother,
        Come riding by the stile.

5. "Oh mother, oh mother, a little of your gold,
        And likewise of your fee,
    To keep my body from yonder grave,
        And my neck from the gallows-tree!"

6. "None of my gold now shall you have,
        Nor likewise of my fee;
    For I am come to see you hangd,
        And hanged you shall be."

7. "Oh good Lord Judge, and sweet Lord Judge,
        Peace for a little while!
    Methinks I see my own brother,
        Come riding by the stile.

8. "Oh brother, oh brother, a little of your gold,
        And likewise of your fee,
    To keep my body from yonder grave,
        And my neck from the gallows-tree!"

9. "None of my gold now shall you have,
        Nor likewise of my fee;
    For I am come to see you hangd,
        And hanged you shall be."

10. "Oh good Lord Judge, and sweet Lord Judge,
        Peace for a little while!

Methinks I see my own sister,
  Come riding by the stile.

11. "Oh sister, oh sister, a little of your gold,
    And likewise of your fee,
  To keep my body from yonder grave,
    And my neck from the gallows-tree!"

12. "None of my gold now shall you have,
    Nor likewise of my fee;
  For I am come to see you hangd,
    And hanged you shall be."

13. "Oh good Lord Judge, and sweet Lord Judge,
    Peace for a little while!
  Methinks I see my own true-love,
    Come riding by the stile.

14. "Oh true-love, oh true-love, a little of your gold,
    And likewise of your fee,
  To save my body from yonder grave,
    And my neck from the gallows-tree."

15. "Some of my gold now you shall have,
    And likewise of my fee,
  For I am come to see you saved,
    And saved you shall be."

XXXII

The Gay Goshawk

The heroine of *The Gay Goshawk* can be compared with Juliet, but in her case the opiate serves its turn. It is a gay, almost mocking ballad, influenced perhaps by a French ballad on a similar theme. The goshawk reminds one of the lover who can take the guise of a falcon or another bird, as in the late ballad of *The Earl of Mar's Daughter*, and in many folk-tales.

1. "O well's me o my gay goss-hawk,
    That he can speak and flee;
   He'll carry a letter to my love,
    Bring back another to me."

2. "O how can I your true-love ken,
    Or how can I her know?
   Whan frae her mouth I never heard couth,
    Nor wi my eyes her saw."

3. "O well sal ye my true-love ken,
    As soon as you her see;
   For, of a' the flowrs in fair Englan,
    The fairest flowr is she.

4. "At even at my love's bowr-door
    There grows a bowing birk,
   An sit ye down and sing thereon,
    As she gangs to the kirk.

5. "An four-and-twenty ladies fair
    Will wash and go to kirk,
   But well shall ye my true-love ken,
    For she wears goud on her skirt.

6. "An four and twenty gay ladies
    Will to the mass repair,

But well sal ye my true-love ken,
 For she wears goud on her hair."

7. O even at that lady's bowr-door
 There grows a bowin birk,
An he set down and sang thereon,
 As she ged to the kirk.

8. "O eet and drink, my marys a',
 The wine flows you among,
Till I gang to my shot-window,
 An hear yon bonny bird's song.

9. "Sing on, sing on, my bonny bird,
 The song ye sang the streen,
For I ken by your sweet singin
 You're frae my true-love sen."

10. O first he sang a merry song,
 An then he sang a grave,
An then he peckd his feathers gray,
 To her the letter gave.

11. "Ha, there's a letter frae your love,
 He says he sent you three;
He canna wait your love langer,
 But for your sake he'll die.

12. "He bids you write a letter to him;
 He says he's sent you five;
He canno wait your love langer,
 Tho you're the fairest woman alive."

13. "Ye bid him bake his bridal-bread,
 And brew his bridal-ale,
An I'll meet him in fair Scotlan
 Lang, lang or it be stale."

14. She's doen her to her father dear,
      Fa'n low down on her knee:
   "A boon, a boon my father dear,
      I pray you, grant it me."

15. "Ask on, ask on, my daughter,
      An granted it sal be;
   Except ae squire in fair Scotlan,
      An him you sall never see."

16. "The only boon, my father dear,
      That I do crave of the,
   Is, gin I die in southin lands,
      In Scotland to bury me.

17. "An the firstin kirk that ye come till,
      Ye gar the bells be rung,
   An the nextin kirk that ye come till,
      Ye gar the mess be sung.

18. "An the thirdin kirk that ye come till,
      You deal gold for my sake,
   An the fourthin kirk that ye come till,
      You tarry there till night."

19. She is doen her to her bigly bowr,
      As fast she she coud fare,
   An she has tane a sleepy draught,
      That she had mixed wi care.

20. She's laid her down upon her bed,
      An soon she's fa'n asleep,
   And soon oer every tender limb
      Cauld death began to creep.

21. Whan night was flown, an day was come,
      Nae ane that did her see

But thought she was as surely dead
    As ony lady coud be.

22. Her father an her brothers dear
    Gard make to her a bier;
The tae half was o guide red gold,
    The tither o silver clear.

23. Her mither an her sisters fair
    Gard work for her a sark;
The tae half was o cambrick fine,
    The tither o needle wark.

24. The firstin kirk that they came till,
    They gard the bells be rung,
An the nextin kirk that they came till,
    They gard the mess be sung.

25. The thirdin kirk that they came till,
    They dealt gold for her sake,
An the fourthin kirk that they came till,
    Lo, there they met her make!

26. "Lay down, lay down the bigly bier,
    Lat me the dead look on;"
Wi cherry cheeks and ruby lips
    She lay an smil'd on him.

27. "O ae sheave o your bread, true-love,
    An ae glass o your wine,
For I hae fasted for your sake
    These fully days is nine.

28. "Gang hame, gang hame, my seven bold brothers,
    Gang hame and sound your horn;
An ye may boast in southin lans
    Your sister's playd you scorn."

XXXIII

Katharine Jaffray

This joyous ballad, the ancestor of Scott's *Lochinvar*, should be compared with the more sombre themes of *The Lady of Arngosk* and *Rob Roy*. Danish and Scandinavian ballads of this type have been shown to be based on historical fact.

1. There livd a lass in yonder dale,
       And doun in yonder glen, O
   And Kathrine Jaffray was her name,
       Well known by many men. O

2. Out came the Laird of Lauderdale,
       Out frae the South Countrie,
   All for to court this pretty maid,
       Her bridegroom for to be.

3. He has teld her father and mither baith,
       And a' the rest o her kin,
   And has teld the lass hersell,
       And her consent has win.

4. Then came the Laird of Lochinton,
       Out frae the English border,
   All for to court this pretty maid,
       Well mounted in good order.

5. He's teld her father and mither baith,
       As I hear sindry say,
   But he has nae teld the lass her sell,
       Till on her wedding day.

6. When day was set, and friends were met,
       And married to be,
   Lord Lauderdale came to the place,
       The bridal for to see.

7. "O are you came for sport, young man?
   Or are you come for play?
   Or are you come for a sight o our bride,
   Just on her wedding day?"

8. "I'm nouther come for sport," he says,
   "Nor am I come for play;
   But if I had one sight o your bride,
   I'll mount and ride away."

9. There was a glass of the red wine
   Filld up them atween,
   And ay she drank to Lauderdale,
   Wha her true-love had been.

10. Then he took her by the milk-white hand,
    And by the grass-green sleeve,
    And he mounted her high behind him there,
    At the bridegroom he askt nae leive.

11. Then the blude run down by the Cowden Banks,
    And down by Cowden Braes,
    And ay she gard the trumpet sound,
    "O this is foul, foul play!"

12. Now a' ye that in England are,
    Or are in England born,
    Come nere to Scotland to court a lass,
    Or else ye'l get the scorn.

13. They haik ye up and settle ye by,
    Till on your wedding day,
    And gie ye frogs instead o fish,
    And play ye foul, foul play.

HISTORICAL BALLADS

XXXIV

Robin Hood and Little John

The tale of how Robin Hood first encountered his most loyal friend and inseparable companion deserves pride of place in our selection. Unfortunately the text of the ballad is preserved only in seventeenth-century prints, but the encounter by the brook is good ballad narrative.

1. When Robin Hood was about twenty years old,
   With a hey down down and a down
   He happend to meet Little John,
   A jolly brisk blade, right fit for the trade,
   For he was a lusty young man.

2. Tho he was calld Little, his limbs they were large,
   And his stature was seven foot high;
   Where-ever he came, they quak'd at his name,
   For soon he would make them to fly.

3. How they came acquainted, I'll tell you in brief,
   If you will but listen a while;
   For this very jest, amongst all the rest,
   I think it may cause you to smile.

4. Bold Robin Hood said to his jolly bowmen,
   Pray tarry you here in this grove;
   And see that you all observe well my call,
   While thorough the forest I rove.

5. We have had no sport for these fourteen long days,
   Therefore now abroad will I go;
   Now should I be beat, and cannot retreat,
   My horn I will presently blow.

6. Then did he shake hands with his merry men all,
   And bid them at present good b'w'ye;
   Then, as near a brook his journey he took,
   A stranger he chancd to espy.

7. They happend to meet on a long narrow bridge,
   And neither of them would give way;
   Quoth bold Robin Hood, and sturdily stood,
   I'll show you right Nottingham play.

8. With that from his quiver an arrow he drew,
   A broad arrow with a goose-wing:
   The stranger reply'd, I'll liquor thy hide,
   If thou offerst to touch the string.

9. Quoth bold Robin Hood, Thou dost prate like an ass,
   For were I to bend but my bow,
   I could send a dart quite thro thy proud heart,
   Before thou couldst strike me one blow.

10. "Thou talkst like a coward," the stranger reply'd;
    "Well armd with a long bow you stand,
    To shoot at my breast, while I, I protest,
    Have nought but a staff in my hand."

11. "The name of a coward," quoth Robin, "I scorn,
    Wherefore my long bow I'll lay by;
    And now, for thy sake, a staff will I take,
    The truth of thy manhood to try."

12. Then Robin Hood stept to a thicket of trees,
    And chose him a staff of ground-oak;
    Now this being done, away he did run
    To the stranger, and merrily spoke:

13. "Lo! see my staff, it is lusty and tough,
    Now here on the bridge we will play;

Whoever falls in, the other shall win
    The battel, and so we'll away."

14. "With all my whole heart," the stranger reply'd;
    "I scorn in the least to give out;"
This said, they fell to 't without more dispute,
    And their staffs they did flourish about.

15. And first Robin he gave the stranger a bang,
    So hard that it made his bones ring;
The stranger he said, "This must be repaid,
    I'll give you as good as you bring.

16. "So long as I'm able to handle my staff,
    To die in your debt, friend, I scorn:"
Then to it each goes, and followd their blows,
    As if they had been threshing of corn.

17. The stranger gave Robin a crack on the crown,
    Which caused the blood to appear;
Then Robin, enrag'd, more fiercely engag'd,
    And followd his blows more severe.

18. So thick and so fast did he lay it on him,
    With a passionate fury and ire,
At every stroke, he made him to smoke,
    As if he had been all on fire.

19. O then into fury the stranger he grew,
    And gave him a damnable look,
And with it a blow that laid him full low,
    And tumbld him into the brook.

20. "I prithee, good fellow, O where art thou now?"
    The stranger, in laughter, he cry'd;
Quoth bold Robin Hood, "Good faith, in the flood,
    And floating along with the tide.

21. "I needs must acknowledge thou art a brave soul;
     With thee I'll no longer contend;
     For needs must I say, thou hast got the day,
     Our battel shall be at an end."

22. Then unto the bank he did presently wade,
     And pulld himself out by a thorn;
     Which done, at the last, he blowd a loud blast
     Straitway on his fine bugle-horn.

23. The eccho of which through the vallies did fly,
     At which his stout bowmen appeard,
     All cloathed in green, most gay to be seen;
     So up to their master they steerd.

24. "O what's the matter?" quoth William Stutely;
     "Good master, you are wet to the skin:"
     "No matter," quoth he; "the lad which you see,
     "In fighting, hath tumbld me in."

25. "He shall not go scot-free," the others reply'd;
     So strait they were seizing him there,
     To duck him likewise; but Robin Hood cries,
     "He is a stout fellow, forbear."

26. "There's no one shall wrong thee, friend, be not afraid;
     These bowmen upon me do wait;
     There's threescore and nine; if thou wilt be mine,
     Thou shalt have my livery strait.

27. "And other accoutrements fit for a man;
     Speak up, jolly blade, never fear;
     I'll teach you also the use of the bow,
     To shoot at the fat fallow-deer."

28. "O here is my hand," the stranger reply'd,
     "I'll serve you with all my whole heart;

My name is John Little, a man of good mettle;
  Nere doubt me, for I'll play my part."

29. "His name shall be alterd," quoth William Stutely,
  "And I will his godfather be;
Prepare then a feast, and none of the least,
  For we will be merry," quoth he.

30. They presently fetchd in a brace of fat does,
  With humming strong liquor likewise;
They lovd what was good; so, in the greenwood,
  This pretty sweet babe they baptize.

31. He was, I must tell you, but seven foot high,
  And, may be, an ell in the waste;
A pretty sweet lad; much feasting they had;
  Bold Robin the christning grac'd.

32. With all his bowmen, which stood in a ring,
  And were of the Notti[n]gham breed;
Brave Stutely comes then, with seven yeomen,
  And did in this manner proceed.

33. "This infant was called John Little," quoth he,
  "Which name shall be changed anon;
The words we'll transpose, so where-ever he goes,
  His name shall be calld Little John."

34. They all with a shout made the elements ring,
  So soon as the office was ore;
To feasting they went, with true merriment,
  And tippld strong liquor gillore.

35. Then Robin he took the pretty sweet babe,
  And cloathd him from top to the toe
In garments of green, most gay to be seen,
  And gave him a curious long bow.

36. "Thou shalt be an archer as well as the best,
    And range in the greenwood with us;
   Where we'll not want gold nor silver, behold,
   While bishops have ought in their purse.

37. "We live here like squires, or lords of renown,
    Without ere a foot of free land;
   We feast on good cheer, with wine, ale, and beer,
   And evry thing at our command."

38. Then musick and dancing did finish the day;
    At length, when the sun waxed low,
   Then all the whole train the grove did refrain,
   And unto their caves they did go.

39. And so ever after, as long as he livd,
    Altho he was proper and tall,
   Yet nevertheless, the truth to express,
   Still Little John they did him call.

XXXV

Robin Hood and the Monk

This ballad is extant in a Cambridge MS. of about 1450, and is thus one of our earliest literary documents of Robin Hood. Little John and Much the Miller's Son are there, and the scene is set in Sherwood Forest and Nottingham. There is a certain roughness and violence in the story which later ages polished away. Two lines are missing in stanza thirty, which may have narrated how Robin Hood's band was told of his capture. The ballad is strong and lively, the prison-break is swiftly told, and the narratives moves with vigorous speed.

1. In somer, when þe shawes be sheyne,
    And leves be large and long,
   Hit is full mery in feyre foreste
   To here þe foulys song:

2. To se þe dere draw to þe dale,
   And leve þe hilles hee,
   And shadow hem in þe levës grene,
   Vnder the grene-wode tre.

3. Hit befel on Whitsontide,
   Erly in a May mornyng,
   The son vp feyre can shyne,
   And the briddis mery can syng.

4. "This is a mery mornyng," seid Litull John,
   "Be hym þat dyed on tre;
   A more mery man þen I am one
   Lyves not in Cristiantë.

5. "Pluk vp þi hert, my dere mayster,"
   Litull John can sey,
   "And thynk hit is a full fayre tyme
   In a mornyng of May."

6. "ʒe, on thyng greves me," seid Robyn,
   "And does my hert mych woo;
   þat I may not no solem day
   To mas nor matyns goo.

7. "Hit is a fourtnet and more," seid he,
   "Syn I my sauyour see;
   To day wil I to Notyngham," seid Robyn,
   "With þe myght of mylde Marye."

8. Than spake Moche, þe mylner sun,
   Euer more wel hym betyde!
   "Take twelue of þi wyght ʒemen,
   Well weppynd, be þi side.
   Such on wolde þi selfe slon,
   þat twelue dar not abyde."

9. "Of all my mery men," seid Robyn,
   "Be my feith I wil non haue,
But Litull John shall beyre my bow,
   Til þat me list to drawe."

10. "þou shall beyre þin own," seid Litull Jon,
   "Maister, and I wyl beyre myne,
And we well shete a peny," seid Litull Jon,
   "Vnder þe grene-wode lyne."

11. "I will not shete a peny," seyd Robyn Hode,
   "In feith, Litull John, with the,
But euer for on as þou shetis," seide Robyn,
   "In feith I holde þe thre."

12. Thus shet þei forth, þese ȝemen too,
   Bothe at buske and brome,
Til Litull John wan of his maister
   Fiue shillings to hose and shone.

13. A ferly strife fel þem betwene,
   As they went bi the wey;
Litull John seid he had won fiue shillings,
   And Robyn Hode seid schortly nay.

14. With þat Robyn Hode lyed Litul Jon,
   And smote hym with his hande;
Litul Jon waxed wroth þerwith,
   And pulled out his bright bronde.

15. "Were þou not my maister," seid Litull John,
   "þou shuldis by hit ful sore;
Get þe a man wher þou w[ilt],
   For þou getis me no more."

16. þen Robyn goes to Notyngham,
   Hym selfe mornyng allone,

And Litull John to mery Scherwode,
   The pathes he knew ilkone.

17. Whan Robyn came to Notyngham,
       Sertenly withouten layn,
   He prayed to God and myld Mary,
       To bryng hym out saue agayn.

18. He gos in to Seynt Mary chirch,
       And kneled down before the rode;
   Alle þat euer were þe church within
       Beheld wel Robyn Hode.

19. Beside hym stod a gret-hedid munke,
       I pray to God woo he be!
   Fful sone he knew gode Robyn,
       As sone as he hym se.

20. Out at þe durre he ran,
       Fful sone and anon;
   Alle þe ȝatis of Notyngham
       He made to be sparred euerychon.

21. "Rise vp," he seid, "þou prowde schereff,
       Buske þe and make þe bowne;
   I haue spyed þe kynggis felon,
       Ffor sothe he is in þis town.

22. "I haue spyed þe false felon,
       As he stondis at his masse;
   Hit is long of þe," seide þe munke,
       "And euer he fro vs passe.

23. "þis traytur name is Robyn Hode,
       Vnder þe grene-wode lynde;
   He robbyt me onys of a hundred pound,
       Hit shalle neuer out of my mynde."

24. Vp þen rose þis prowde shereff
    And radly made hym ȝare;
    Many was þe moder son
    To þe kyrk with hym can fare.

25. In at þe durres þei throly thrast,
    With staves ful gode wone;
    "Alas, alas!" seid Robyn Hode,
    "Now mysse I Litull John."

26. But Robyn toke out a too-hond sworde,
    þat hangit down be his kne;
    þer as þe shereff and his men stode thyckust,
    Thedurwarde wolde he.

27. Thryes thorowout þem he ran þen,
    For soþe as I yow sey,
    And woundyt mony a moder son,
    And twelue he slew þat day.

28. His sworde vpon þe schireff hed
    Sertanly he brake in too;
    "þe smyth þat þe made," seid Robyn,
    "I pray to God wyrke hym woo!

29. "Ffor now am I weppynlesse," seid Robyn,
    "Alasse! agayn my wylle;
    But if I may fle þese traytors fro,
    I wot þei wil me kyll."

30. Robyn in to the churchë ran,
    Throout hem euerilkon,

    *   *   *   *   *

31. Sum fel in swonyng as þei were dede,
    And lay stil as any stone;

Non of theym were in her mynde
But only Litull Jon.

32. "Let be your rule," seid Litull Jon,
 "Ffor his luf þat dyed on tre,
 ȝe þat shulde be duȝty men;
 Het is gret shame to se.

33. "Oure maister has bene hard bystode
 And ȝet scapyd away;
 Pluk vp your hertis, and leve þis mone,
 And harkyn what I shal say.

34. "He has seruyd Oure Lady many a day,
 And ȝet wil, securly;
 þerfor I trust in hir specialy
 No wyckud deth shal he dye.

35. "þerfor be glad," seid Litul John,
 "And let þis mournyng be;
 And I shal be þe munkis gyde,
 With þe myght of mylde Mary.

36. .   .   .   .   .
 "We will go but we too;
 And I mete hym," seid Litul John,
 .   .   .   .   .

37. "Loke þat ȝe kepe wel owre tristil-tre,
 Vnder þe levys smale,
 And spare non of this venyson,
 þat gose in thys vale."

38. Fforþe þen went these ȝemen too,
 Litul John and Moche on fere,
 And lokid on Moch emys hows,
 þe hye way lay full nere.

39. Litul John stode at a wyndow in þe mornyng,
  And lokid forþ at a stage;
  He was war wher þe munke came ridyng,
    And with hym a litul page.

40. "Be my feith," seid Litul John to Moch,
  "I can þe tel tithyngus gode;
  I se wher þe munke cumys rydyng,
    I know hym be his wyde hode."

41. They went in to the way, þese ȝemen boþe,
  As curtes men and hende;
  þei spyrred tithyngus at þe munke,
    As they hade bene his frende.

42. "Ffro whens come ȝe?" seid Litull Jon,
  "Tel vs tithyngus, I yow pray,
  Off a false owtlay, [callid Robyn Hode,]
    Was takyn ȝisterday.

43. "He robbyt me and my felowes boþe
  Of twenti marke in serten;
  If þat false owtlay be takyn,
    Ffor soþe we wolde be fayn."

44. "So did he me," seid þe munke,
  "Of a hundred pound and more;
  I layde furst hande hym apon,
    ȝe may thonke me þerfore."

45. "I pray God thanke you," seid Litull John,
  "And we wil when we may;
  We wil go with you, with your leve,
    And bryng yow on your way.

46. "Ffor Robyn Hode hase many a wilde felow,
  I tell you in certen;

If þei wist ʒe rode þis way,
    In feith ʒe shulde be slayn."

47. As þei went talking be þe way,
    The munke and Litull John,
John toke þe munkis horse be þe hede,
    Fful sone and anon.

48. Johne toke þe munkis horse be þe hed,
    Ffor soþe as I yow say;
So did Much þe litull page,
    Ffor he shulde not scape away.

49. Be þe golett of þe hode
    John pulled þe munke down;
John was nothyng of hym agast,
    He lete hym falle on his crown.

50. Litull John was so[re] agrevyd,
    And drew owt his swerde in hye;
This munke saw he shulde be ded,
    Lowd mercy can he crye.

51. "He was my maister," seid Litull John,
    "þat þou hase browʒt in bale;
Shalle þou neuer cum at our kyng,
    Ffor to telle hym tale."

52. John smote of þe munkis hed,
    No longer wolde he dwell;
So did Moch þe litull page,
    Ffor ferd lest he wolde tell.

53. þer þei beryed hem boþe,
    In nouþer mosse nor lyng,
And Litull John and Much infere
    Bare þe letturs to oure kyng.

54.   .   .   .   .   .   .
      He knelid down vpon his kne:
   "God ȝow saue, my lege lorde,
      Ihesus yow saue and se!

55. "God yow saue, my lege kyng!"
      To speke John was full bolde;
   He gaf hym þe letturs in his hond,
      The kyng did hit vnfold.

56. þe kyng red þe letturs anon,
      And seid, So mot I the,
   þer was neuer ȝoman in mery Inglond
      I longut so sore to se.

57. "Wher is þe munke þat þese shuld haue brouȝt?"
      Oure kyng can say:
   "Be my trouth," seid Litull John,
      "He dyed after þe way."

58. þe kyng gaf Moch and Litul Jon
      Twenti pound in sertan,
   And made þeim ȝemen of þe crown,
      And bade þeim go agayn.

59. He gaf John þe seel in hand,
      The sheref for to bere,
   To bryng Robyn hym to,
      And no man do hym dere.

60. John toke his leve at oure kyng,
      þe sothe as I yow say;
   þe next way to Notyngham
      To take, he ȝede þe way.

61. Whan John came to Notyngham
      The ȝatis were sparred ychon;

John callid vp þe porter,
He answerid sone anon.

62. "What is þe cause," seid Litul Jon,
    "þou sparris þe ȝates so fast?"
  "Because of Robyn Hode," seid [þe] porter,
    "In depe prison is cast.

63. "John and Moch and Wyll Scathlok,
    Ffor sothe as I yow say,
  þei slew oure men vpon our wallis,
    And sawten vs euery day."

64. Litull John spyrred after þe schereff,
    And sone he hym fonde;
  He oppyned þe kyngus priue seell,
    And gaf hym in his honde.

65. Whan þe scheref saw þe kyngus seell,
    He did of his hode anon:
  "Wher is þe munke þat bare þe letturs?"
    He seid to Litull John.

66. "He is so fayn of hym," seid Litul John,
    "Ffor soþe as I yow say,
  He has made hym abot of Westmynster,
    A lorde of þat abbay."

67. The scheref made John gode chere,
    And gaf hym wyne of the best;
  At nyȝt þei went to her bedde,
    And euery man to his rest.

68. When þe scheref was on slepe,
    Dronken of wyne and ale,
  Litul John and Moch for soþe
    Toke þe way vnto þe jale.

69. Litul John callid vp þe jayler,
       And bade hym rise anon;
    He seyd Robyn Hode had brokyn prison,
       And out of hit was gon.

70. The porter rose anon sertan,
       As sone as he herd John calle;
    Litul John was redy with a swerd,
       And bare hym to þe walle.

71. "Now wil I be porter," seid Litul John,
       "And take þe keyes in honde:"
    He toke þe way to Robyn Hode,
       And sone he hym vnbonde.

72. He gaf hym a gode swerd in his hond,
       His hed [ther]with for to kepe,
    And ther as þe walle was lowyst
       Anon down can þei lepe.

73. Be þat þe cok began to crow,
       The day began to spryng;
    The scheref fond þe jaylier ded,
       The comyn bell made he ryng.

74. He made a crye thoroout al þe tow[n],
       Wheder he be ȝoman or knave,
    þat cowþe bryng hym Robyn Hode,
       His warison he shuld haue.

75. "Ffor I dar neuer," said þe scheref,
       "Cum before oure kyng;
    Ffor if I do, I wot serten
       Ffor soþe he wil me heng."

76. The scheref made to seke Notyngham,
       Bothe be strete and stye,

And Robyn was in mery Scherwode,
    As liȝt as lef on lynde.

77. Then bespake gode Litull John,
    To Robyn Hode can he say,
I haue done þe a gode turne for an euyll,
    Quyte þe whan þou may.

78. "I haue done þe a gode turne," seid Litull John,
    "Ffor sothe as I yow say;
I haue brouȝt þe vnder grene-wode lyne;
    Ffare wel, and haue gode day."

79. "Nay, be my trouth," seid Robyn Hode,
    "So shall hit neuer be;
I make þe maister," seid Robyn Hode,
    "Off alle my men and me."

80. "Nay, be my trouth," seid Litull John,
    "So shalle hit neuer be;
But lat me be a felow," seid Litull John,
    "No noder kepe I be."

81. Thus John gate Robyn Hod out of prison,
    Sertan withoutyn layn;
Whan his men saw hym hol and sounde,
    Ffor sothe they were full fayne.

82. They filled in wyne, and made hem glad,
    Vnder þe levys smale,
And ȝete pastes of venyson,
    þat gode was with ale.

83. Than worde came to oure kyng
    How Robyn Hode was gon,
And how þe scheref of Notyngham
    Durst neuer loke hym vpon.

84. Then bespake oure cumly kyng,
        In an angur hye:
    Litull John hase begyled þe schereff,
        In faith so hase he me.

85. Litul John has begyled vs bothe,
        And þat full wel I se;
    Or ellis þe schereff of Notyngham
        Hye hongut shulde he be.

86. "I made hem ȝemen of þe crowne,
        And gaf hem fee with my hond;
    I gaf hem grith," seid oure kyng,
        "Thorowout all mery Inglond.

87. "I gaf theym grith," þen seid oure kyng;
        "I say, so mot I the,
    Ffor sothe soch a ȝeman as he is on
        In all Inglond ar not thre.

88. "He is trew to his maister," seid our kyng;
        "I sey, be swete Seynt John,
    He louys better Robyn Hode
        Then he dose vs ychon.

89. "Robyn Hode is euer bond to hym,
        Bothe in strete and stalle:
    Speke no more of this mater," seid oure kyng,
        "But John has begyled vs alle."

90. Thus endys the talkyng of the munke
        And Robyn Hode i-wysse;
    God, þat is euer a crowned kyng,
        Bryng vs all to his blisse!

XXXVI

Robin Hood's Death

There are two versions of Robin Hood's death in addition to the short account in the closing stanzas of *A Gest of Robyn Hode*. Of these, the second, inferior version is preserved in late eighteenth-century prints without much poetic interest. Version A, from the Percy Manuscript and of uncertain age, printed here, has two gaps of nine stanzas, one after stanza eight, the other after stanza eighteen. Therefore we shall never know why the old woman curses Robin, or who the mourners are. Nor can we be certain how Red Roger, the friend of the treacherous prioress, and Little John are stationed. The loss of these stanzas is all the more regrettable as *Robin Hood's Death* is a fine tragic ballad about the death of a hero who, like many true heroes (Achilles, Sigurd), can be laid low only by treason.

1. "I will neuer eate nor drinke," Robin Hood said,
   "Nor meate will doo me noe good,
   Till I haue beene att merry Churchlees,
   My vaines for to let blood."

2. "That I reade not," said Will Scarllett,
   "Master, by the assente of me,
   Without halfe a hundred of your best bowmen
   You take to goe with yee.

3. "For there a good yeoman doth abide
   Will be sure to quarrell with thee,
   And if thou haue need of vs, master,
   In faith we will not flee."

4. "And thou be feard, thou William Scarlett,
   Att home I read thee bee:"
   "And you be wrothe, my deare master,
   You shall neuer heare more of mee."

   *   *   *   *   *

5. "For there shall noe man with me goe,
       Nor man with mee ryde,
   And Litle Iohn shall be my man,
       And beare my benbow by my side."

6. "You'st beare your bowe, master, your selfe,
       And shoote for a peny with mee:"
   "To that I doe assent," Robin Hood sayd,
       "And soe, Iohn, lett it bee."

7. They two bolde children shotten together,
       All day theire selfe in ranke,
   Vntill they came to blacke water,
       And over it laid a planke.

8. Vpon it there kneeled an old woman,
       Was banning Robin Hoode;
   "Why dost thou bann Robin Hoode?"
       said Robin, . . .

       *   *   *   *   *

9. .   .   .   .   .   .
       "To giue to Robin Hoode;
   Wee weepen for his deare body,
       That this day must be lett bloode."

10. "The dame prior is my aunts daughter,
        And nie vnto my kinne;
    I know shee wold me noe harme this day,
        For all the world to winne."

11. Forth then shotten these children two,
        And they did neuer lin,
    Vntill they came to merry Churchlees,
        To merry Churchlee[s] with-in.

12. And when they came to merry Churchlees,
      They knoced vpon a pin;
   Vpp then rose dame prioresse,
      And lett good Robin in.

13. Then Robin gaue to dame prioresse
      Twenty pound in gold,
   And bad her spend while that wold last,
      And shee shold haue more when shee wold.

14. And downe then came dame prioresse,
      Downe she came in that ilke,
   With a pair off blood-irons in her hands,
      Were wrapped all in silke.

15. "Sett a chaffing-dish to the fyer," said dame prioresse,
      "And stripp thou vp thy sleeue:"
   I hold him but an vnwise man
      That will noe warning leeue.

16. Shee laid the blood-irons to Robin Hoods vaine,
      Alacke, the more pitye!
   And pearct the vaine, and let out the bloode,
      That full red was to see.

17. And first it bled, the thicke, thicke bloode,
      And afterwards the thinne,
   And well then wist good Robin Hoode
      Treason there was within.

18. "What cheere my master?" said Litle Iohn;
      'In faith, Iohn, litle goode;"

      .   .   .   .   .   .

         .   .   .   .   .   .

   *   *   *   *   *   *

19. "I haue upon a gowne of greene,
    Is cut short by my knee,
    And in my hand a bright browne brand
    That will well bite of thee."

20. But forth then of a shot-windowe
    Good Robin Hood he could glide;
    Red Roger, with a grounden glaue,
    Thrust him through the milke-white side.

21. But Robin was light and nimble of foote,
    And thought to abate his pride,
    Ffor betwixt his head and his shoulders
    He made a wound full wide.

22. Says, Ly there, ly there, Red Roger,
    The doggs they must thee eate;
    "For I may haue my houzle," he said,
    "For I may both goe and speake.

23. "Now giue me mood," Robin said to Litle Iohn,
    "Giue me mood with thy hand;
    I trust to God in heauen soe hye
    My houzle will me bestand."

24. "Now giue me leaue, giue me leaue, master," he said,
    "For Christs loue giue leaue to me,
    To set a fier within this hall,
    And to burne vp all Churchlee."

25. "That I reade not," said Robin Hoode then,
    "Litle Iohn, for it may not be;
    If I shold doe any widow hurt, at my latter end,
    God," he said, "wold blame me;

26. "But take me vpon thy backe, Litle Iohn,
    And beare me to yonder streete,

And there make me a full fayre graue,
Of grauell and of greete.

27. "And sett my bright sword at my head,
Mine arrowes at my feete,
And lay my vew-bow by my side,
My met-yard wi . . . .

XXXVII

Sir Patrick Spens

The variant given here was first published by Percy in the *Reliques* from two Scottish MS. copies. Other variants with additional stanzas have come to light, explaining the purpose of the mission of the Scottish lords as the wooing of a Norwegian princess for their King, and making it clear that disaster befell them on the journey back to Scotland. But Percy's version is infinitely superior to all the other variants in its compactness, in the swiftness of its narrative, and in the power of its unforgettable conclusion.

Little enough is known about the historical background of *Sir Patrick Spens*: of the hero nothing is known with certainty, and the disaster seems to reflect mishaps connected with two thirteenth-century dynastic marriages, one of them the death of the Maid of Norway on her journey to be married to the eldest son of Edward I of England in 1290.

1. The king sits in Dumferling toune,
Drinking the blude-reid wine:
"O whar will I get guid sailor,
To sail this schip of mine?"

2. Up and spak an eldern knicht,
Sat at the kings richt kne:
"Sir Patrick Spence is the best sailor
That sails upon the se."

3. The king has written a braid letter,
And signd it wi his hand,

And sent it to Sir Patrick Spence,
　　Was walking on the sand.

4. The first line that Sir Patrick red,
　　　A loud lauch lauched he;
　　The next line that Sir Patrick red,
　　　The teir blinded his ee.

5. "O wha is this has don this deid,
　　　This ill deid don to me,
　　To send me out this time o' the yeir,
　　　To sail upon the se!

6. "Mak hast, mak haste, my mirry men all,
　　　Our guid schip sails the morne:"
　　"O say na sae, my master deir,
　　　For I feir a deadlie storme.

7. "Late late yestreen I saw the new moone,
　　　Wi the auld moone in hir arme,
　　And I feir, I feir, my deir master,
　　　That we will cum to harme."

8. O our Scots nobles wer richt laith
　　　To weet their cork-heild schoone;
　　Bot lang owre a' the play wer playd,
　　　Thair hats they swam aboone.

9. O lang, lang may their ladies sit,
　　　Wi thair fans into their hand,
　　Or eir they se Sir Patrick Spence
　　　Cum sailing to the land.

10. O lang, lang may the ladies stand,
　　　Wi thair gold kems in their hair,
　　Waiting for thair ain deir lords,
　　　For they'll se thame na mair.

11. Haf owre, haf owre to Aberdour,
        It's fiftie fadom deip,
    And thair lies guid Sir Patrick Spence,
        Wi the Scots lords at his feit.

XXXVIII

Johnie Cock

Where Robin Hood outwits gamekeepers and foresters, and feasts of
the venison to his heart's delight, Johnie Cock pays dearly. Nothing
more than this fine ballad tells us is known of him, but how one's heart
warms to his courage and to his bearing in his last struggle. An elegiac
note, alien to the Robin Hood cycle, except in *Robin Hood's Death*, re-
inforces this stress on the hero's courage: Johnie is 'fey,' and his mother's
apprehension, the ghostly figure of the old palmer, the surfeit of deer
flesh, and the seven foresters in their hiding-place are the perfect expression of his doom. Remembering "Ald Carl Hood" in *Earl Brand*, one
wonders whether the old palmer may not be Odhin, calling a favourite
hero to join the company of the immortals.

1. Johny he has risen up i the morn,
        Calls for water to wash his hands;
    But little knew he that his bloody hounds
        Were bound in iron bands.   bands
        Were bound in iron bands

2. Johny's mother has gotten word o that,
        And care-bed she has taen:
    "O Johny, for my benison,
        I beg you'l stay at hame;
    For the wine so red, and the well baken bread,
        My Johny shall want nane.

3. "There are seven forsters at Pickeram Side,
        At Pickeram where they dwell,
    And for a drop of thy heart's bluid
        They wad ride the fords of hell."

4. Johny he's gotten word of that,
   And he's turnd wondrous keen;
He's put off the red scarlett,
   And he's put on the Lincolm green.

5. With a sheaf of arrows by his side,
   And a bent bow in his hand,
He's mounted on a prancing steed,
   And he has ridden fast oer the strand

6. He's up i Braidhouplee, and down i Bradyslee,
   And under a buss o broom,
And there he found a good dun deer,
   Feeding in a buss of ling.

7. Johny shot, and the dun deer lap,
   And she lap wondrous wide,
Until they came to the wan water,
   And he stemd her of her pride.

8. He 'as taen out the little pen-knife,
   'T was full three quarters long,
And he has taen out of that dun deer
   The liver bot and the tongue.

9. They eat of the flesh, and they drank of the blood,
   And the blood it was so sweet,
Which caused Johny and his bloody hounds
   To fall in a deep sleep.

10. By then came an old palmer,
    And an ill death may he die!
For he's away to Pickram Side,
    As fast as he can drie.

11. "What news, what news?" says the Seven Forsters,
    "What news have ye brought to me?"

"I have noe news," the palmer said,
    "But what I saw with my eye.

12. "High up i Bradyslee, low down i Bradisslee,
    And under a buss of scroggs,
O there I spied a well-wight man,
    Sleeping among his dogs.

13. "His coat it was of light Lincolm,
    And his breeches of the same,
His shoes of the American leather,
    And gold buckles tying them."

14. Up bespake the Seven Forsters,
    Up bespake they ane and a':
O that is Johny o Cockleys Well,
    And near him we will draw.

15. O the first y stroke that they gae him,
    They struck him off by the knee;
Then up bespake his sister's son:
    "O the next'll gar him die!"

16. "O some they count ye well-wight men,
    But I do count ye nane;
For you might well ha wakend me,
    And askd gin I wad be taen.

17. "The wildest wolf in aw this wood
    Wad not ha done so by me;
She'd ha wet her foot ith wan water,
    And sprinkled it oer my brae,
And if that wad not ha wakend me,
    She wad ha gone and let me be.

18. "O bows of yew, if ye be true,
    In London, where ye were bought,

> Fingers five, get up belive,
>   Manhuid shall fail me nought."

19. He has killd the Seven Forsters,
>   He has killd them all but ane,
>   And that wan scarce to Pickeram Side,
>   To carry the bode-words hame.

20. "Is there never a boy in a' this wood
>   That will tell what I can say;
>   That will go to Cockleys Well,
>   Tell my mither to fetch me away?"

21. There was a boy into that wood,
>   That carried the tidings away,
>   And many ae was the well-wight man
>   At the fetching o Johny away.

XXXIX

The Hunting of the Cheviot
(Chevy Chase)

The Battle of Otterburn was fought on August 19, 1388, during the reign of Richard II, and not, as *The Hunting of the Cheviot* declares, of Henry IV. Both this ballad and *The Battle of Otterburn* were current by 1549, as they are mentioned in *The Complaynt of Scotland*. Sir E. K. Chambers (*English Literature at the Close of the Middle Ages*, p. 162)[1] suggests that the earliest forms of the ballads were composed by minstrels some time before 1549.

The Hunting of the Cheviot (or *Chevy Chase*) has enjoyed extraordinary popularity among the very best judges of poetry. Sir Philip Sidney never heard it without his chivalrous heart being "mooued more then with a Trumpet." Ben Jonson would rather have been the author of *Chevy Chase* than of all his works. Addison devoted two fine critical essays

[1] Oxford University Press, 1945.

(*Spectator*, Nos. 70, 74) to the ballad. Something of our Anglo-Saxon heritage, of the spirit that informs Beowulf in his fight against the dragon or of the high endeavour of the Battles of Brunnanburh and Maldon, survives in these poems. The challenge under the walls of Newcastle-upon-Tyne, with Percy's chivalrous gesture of handing a pipe of wine to his enemies, the lovely scene of the hunting of the deer, the roll-call of noble names before the battle, and, above all, the actual battle scenes—in all these we sense the heroic and chivalrous ideals of the age. Small touches adding strength to the complete picture abound. Percy's offer to decide the battle by a duel with Douglas, the sturdy self-assurance of the squire who refuses to stand aside, the slow-motion effect of the description of the arrow-shot that kills Sir Hugh Montgomery, the contrast between swordsmanship and archery—all these imaginative details give validity to the central theme. The language of both poems, with its stock phrases, its stately and unhurried progress, and its general plasticity adds to the greatness of these ballads. It is worth noting that the authors of the two ballads clearly worked on somewhat varying reports of the battle.

1. The Persë owt off Northombarlonde,
    and avowe to God mayd he
  That he wold hunte in the mowntayns
    off Chyviat within days thre,
  In the magger of doughtë Dogles,
    and all that euer with him be.

2. The fattiste hartes in all Cheviat
    he sayd he wold kyll, and cary them away:
  "Be my feth," sayd the dougheti Doglas agayn,
    "I wyll let that hontyng yf that I may."

3. The[n] the Persë owt off Banborowe cam,
    with him a myghtee meany,
  With fiftene hondrith archares bold off blood and
      bone;
  The wear chosen owt of shyars thre.

4. This begane on a Monday at morn,
    in Cheviat the hillys so he;
  The chylde may rue that ys vn-born,
    it wos the mor pittë.

5. The dryvars thorowe the woodës went,
    for to reas the dear;
  Bomen byckarte vppone the bent
    with ther browd aros cleare.

6. Then the wyld thorowe the woodës went,
    on euery sydë shear;
  Greahondes thorowe the grevis glent,
    for to kyll thear dear.

7. This begane in Chyviat the hyls abone,
    yerly on a Monnyn-day;
  Be that it drewe to the oware off none,
    a hondrith fat hartës ded ther lay.

8. The blewe a mort vppone the bent,
    the semblyde on sydis shear;
  To the quyrry then the Persë went,
    to se the bryttlynge off the deare.

9. He sayd, It was the Duglas promys
    this day to met me hear;
  But I wyste he wolde faylle, verament;
    a great oth the Persë swear.

10. At the laste a squyar off Northomberlonde
    lokyde at his hand full ny;
  He was war a the doughetie Doglas commynge,
    with him a myghttë meany.

11. Both with spear, bylle, and brande,
    yt was a myghtti sight to se;
  Hardyar men, both off hart nor hande,
    wear not in Cristiantë.

12. The wear twenti hondrith spear-men good,
    withoute any feale;

The wear borne along be the watter a Twyde,
  yth bowndës of Tividale.

1 3 "Leave of the brytlyng of the dear," he sayd,
    "and to your boÿs lock ye tayk good hede;
  For neuer sithe ye wear on your mothars borne
    had ye neuer so mickle nede."

14. The dougheti Dogglas on a stede,
    he rode alle his men beforne;
  His armor glytteryde as dyd a glede;
    a boldar barne was never born.

15. "Tell me whos men ye ar," he says,
    "or whos men that ye be:
  Who gave youe leave to hunte in this Chyviat chays,
    in the spyt of myn and of me."

16. The first mane that ever him an answear mayd,
    yt was the good lord Persë:
  "We wyll not tell the whoys men we are," he says,
    "nor whos men that we be;
  But we wyll hounte hear in this chays,
    in the spyt of thyne and of the.

17. "The fattiste hartës in all Chyviat
    we haue kyld, and cast to carry them away:"
  "Be my troth," sayd the doghetë Dogglas agay[n],
    "therfor the ton of vs shall de this day."

18. Then sayd the doughtë Doglas
    unto the lord Persë:
  "To kyll alle thes giltles men,
    alas, it wear great pittë!

19. "But, Persë, thowe art a lord of lande,
    I am a yerle callyd within my contrë;

> Let all our men vppone a parti stande,
>   and do the battell off the and of me."

20. "Nowe Cristes cors on his crowne," sayd the lorde
        Persë,
      "who-so-euer ther-to says nay!
    Be my troth, doughttë Doglas," he says,
      "thow shalt neuer se that day.

21. "Nethar in Ynglonde, Skottlonde, nar France,
      nor for no man of a woman born,
    But, and fortune be my chance,
      I dar met him, on man for on."

22. Then bespayke a squyar off Northombarlonde,
      Richard Wytharyngton was him nam;
    "It shall neuer be told in Sothe-Ynglonde," he says,
      "To Kyng Herry the Fourth for sham.

23. "I wat youe byn great lordës twaw,
      I am a poor squyar of lande;
    I wylle neuer se my captayne fyght on a fylde,
      and stande my selffe and loocke on,
    But whylle I may my weppone welde,
      I wylle not [fayle] both hart and hande."

24. That day, that day, that dredfull day!
      the first fit here I fynde;
    And youe wyll here any mor a the hountynge a the
        Chyviat,
      yet ys ther mor behynde.

25. The Yngglyshe men hade ther bowys yebent,
      ther hartes wer good yenoughe;
    The first off arros that the shote off,
      seven skore spear-men the sloughe.

26. Yet byddys the yerle Doglas vppon the bent,
    a captayne good yenoughe,
    And that was sene verament,
    for he wrought hom both woo and wouche.

27. The Dogglas partyd his ost in thre,
    lyk a cheffe cheften off pryde;
    With suar spears off myghttë tre,
    the cum in on euery syde;

28. Thrughe our Yngglyshe archery
    gave many a wounde fulle wyde;
    Many a doughetë the garde to dy,
    which ganyde them no pryde.

29. The Ynglyshe men let ther boÿs be,
    and pulde owt brandes that wer brighte;
    It was a hevy syght to se
    bryght swordes on basnites lyght.

30. Thorowe ryche male and myneyeple,
    many sterne the strocke done streght;
    Many a freyke that was fulle fre,
    ther vndar foot dyd lyght.

31. At last the Duglas and the Persë met,
    lyk to captayns of myght and of mayne;
    The swapte togethar tylle the both swat,
    with swordes that wear of fyn myllan.

32. Thes worthë freckys for to fyght,
    ther-to the wear fulle fayne,
    Tylle the bloode owte off thear basnetes sprente,
    as euer dyd heal or ra[y]n.

33. "Yelde the, Persë," sayde the Doglas,
    "and i feth I shalle the brynge

Wher thowe shalte haue a yerls wagis
   of Jamy our Skottish kynge.

34. "Thoue shalte haue thy ransom fre,
      I hight the hear this thinge;
   For the manfullyste man yet art thowe
      that euer I conqueryd in filde fighttynge."

35. "Nay," sayd the lord Persë,
      "I tolde it the beforne,
   That I wolde neuer yeldyde be
      to no man of a woman born."

36. With that ther cam an arrowe hastely,
      forthe off a myghttë wane;
   Hit hathe strekene the yerle Duglas
      in at the brest-bane.

37. Thorowe lyvar and longës bathe
      the sharpe arrowe ys gane,
   That neuer after in all his lyffe-days
      he spayke mo wordës but ane:
   That was, Fyghte ye, my myrry men, whyllys ye may,
      for my lyff-days ben gan.

38. The Persë leanyde on his brande,
      and sawe the Duglas de;
   He tooke the dede mane by the hande,
      and sayd, Wo ys me for the!

39. "To haue savyde thy lyffe, I wolde haue partyde with
      my landes for years thre,
   For a better man, of hart nare of hande,
      was nat in all the north contrë."

40. Off all that se a Skottishe knyght,
      was callyd Ser Hewe the Monggombyrry;

He sawe the Duglas to the deth was dyght,
   he spendyd a spear, a trusti tre.

41. He rod vppone a corsiare
   throughe a hondrith archerÿ:
He neuer stynttyde, nar neuer blane,
   tylle he cam to the good lord Persë.

42. He set vppone the lorde Persë
   a dynte that was full soare;
With a suar spear of a myghttë tre
   clean thorow the body he the Persë ber,

43. A the tothar syde that a man myght se
   a large cloth-yard and mare;
Towe bettar captayns wear nat in Cristiantë
   then that day slan wear ther.

44. An archar off Northomberlonde
   say slean was the lord Persë;
He bar a bende bowe in his hand,
   was made off trusti tre.

45. An arow that a cloth-yarde was lang
   to the harde stele halyde he;
A dynt that was both sad and soar
   he sat on Ser Hewe the Monggombyrry.

46. The dynt yt was both sad and sar
   that he of Monggomberry sete;
The swane-fethars that his arrowe bar
   with his hart-blood the wear wete.

47. Ther was neuer a freake wone foot wolde fle,
   but still in stour dyd stand,
Heawyng on yche othar, whylle the myghte dre,
   with many a balfull brande.

48. This battell begane in Chyviat
    an owar befor the none,
  And when even-songe bell was rang,
    the battell was nat half done.

49. The tocke ... on ethar hande
    be the lyght off the mone;
  Many hade no strenght for to stande,
    in Chyviat the hillys abon.

50. Of fifteen hondrith archars of Ynglonde
    went away but seuenti and thre;
  Of twenti hondrith spear-men of Skotlonde,
    but even five and fifti.

51. But all wear slayne Cheviat within;
    the hade no streng[th]e to stand on by;
  The chylde may rue that ys unborne,
    it was the mor pittë.

52. Thear was slayne, withe the lord Persë,
    Ser Johan of Agerstone,
  Ser Rogar, the hinde Hartly,
    Ser Wyllyam, the bolde Hearone.

53. Ser Jorg, the worthë Loumle,
    a knyghte of great renowen,
  Ser Raff, the ryche Rugbe,
    with dyntes wear beaten dowene.

54. For Wetharryngton my harte was wo,
    that euer he slayne shulde be;
  For when both his leggis wear hewyne in to,
    yet he knyled and fought on hys kny.

55. Ther was slayne, with the dougheti Duglas,
    Ser Hewe the Monggombyrry,

Ser Dauy Lwadle, that worthë was,
   his sistars son was he.

56. Ser Charls a Murrë in that place,
   that neuer a foot wolde fle;
Ser Hewe Maxwelle, a lorde he was,
   with the Doglas dyd he dey.

57. So on the morrowe the mayde them byears
   off birch and hasell so g[r]ay;
Many wedous, with wepyng tears,
   cam to fache ther makys away.

58. Tivydale may carpe off care,
   Northombarlond may mayk great mon,
For towe such captayns as slayne wear thear
   on the March-parti shall neuer be non.

59. Word ys commen to Eddenburrowe,
   to Jamy the Skottishe kynge,
That dougheti Duglas, lyff-tenant of the Marches,
   he lay slean Chyviot within.

60. His handdës dyd he weal and wryng,
   he sayd, Alas, and woe ys me!
Such an othar captayn Skotland within,
   he sayd, ye-feth shuld neuer be.

61. Worde ys commyn to lovly Londone,
   till the fourth Harry our kynge,
That lord Persë, leyff-tenante of the Marchis,
   he lay slayne Chyviat within.

62. "God haue merci on his solle," sayde Kyng Harry,
   "good lord, yf thy will it be!
I haue a hondrith captayns in Ynglonde," he sayd,
   "as good as euer was he:

But, Persë, and I brook my lyffe,
    thy deth well quyte shall be."

63. As our noble kynge mayd his avowe,
    lyke a noble prince of renowen,
For the deth of the lord Persë
    he dyde the battell of Hombyll-down;

64. Wher syx and thrittë Skottishe knyghtes
    on a day wear beaten down;
Glendale glytteryde on ther armor bryght,
    over castille, towar, and town.

65. This was the hontynge off the Cheviat,
    That tear begane this spurn;
Old men that knowen the grownde well yenoughe
    call it the battell of Otterburn.

66. At Otterburn begane this spurne,
    vppone a Monnynday;
Ther was the doughtë Doglas slean,
    the Persë neuer went away

67. Ther was neuer a tym on the Marchepartës
    sen the Doglas and the Persë met,
But yt ys mervele and the rede blude ronne not,
    as the reane doys in the stret.

68. Ihesue Crist our balys bete,
    and to the blys vs brynge!
Thus was the hountynge of the Chivyat:
    God send vs alle good endyng!

XL

The Battle of Harlaw

A spirited ballad about the defeat of a raiding Highland force by men of the Lowlands in 1411. A ballad on the subject is mentioned in *The Complaynt of Scotland* (1549), but the ballad below was obtained in 1888 in Aberdeenshire, the scene of the battle. The ballad imitates in part the Scots of a Highland speaker.

1. As I cam in by Dunidier,
    An doun by Netherha,
   There was fifty thousand Hielanmen
    A-marching to Harlaw.
   Wi a dree dree dradie drumtie dree.

2. As I cam on, an farther on,
    An doun an by Balquhain,
   Oh there I met Sir James the Rose,
    Wi him Sir John the Gryme.

3. "O cam ye frae the Hielans man?
    An cam ye a' the wey?
   Saw ye Macdonell an his men,
    As they cam frae the Skee?"

4. "Yes, me cam frae ta Hielans, man,
    An me cam a' ta wey,
   An she saw Macdonell an his men,
    As they cam frae ta Skee."

5. "Oh was ye near Macdonell's men?
    Did ye their numbers see?
   Come, tell to me, John Hielanman,
    What micht their numbers be?"

6. "Yes, me was near, an near eneuch,
    An me their numbers saw;

There was fifty thousan Hielanmen
　　A-marchin to Harlaw."

7. "Gin that be true," says James the Rose,
　　" We'll no come meikle speed;
We'll cry upo our merry men,
　　And lichtly mount our steed."

8. "Oh no, oh no," says John the Gryme,
　　" That thing maun never be;
The gallant Grymes were never bate,
　　We'll try phat we can dee."

9. As I cam on, an farther on,
　　An doun an by Harlaw,
They fell fu close on ilka side;
　　Sie fun ye never saw.

10. They fell fu close on ilka side,
　　Sic fun ye never saw;
For Hielan swords gied clash for clash
　　At the battle o Harlaw.

11. The Hielanmen, wi their lang swords,
　　They laid on us fu sair,
An they drave back our merry men
　　Three acres breadth an mair.

12. Brave Forbës to his brither did say,
　　Noo brither, dinna ye see?
They beat us back on ilka side,
　　An we'se be forced to flee.

13. "Oh no, oh no, my brither dear,
　　That thing maun never be;
Tak ye your good sword in your hand,
　　An come your wa's wi me."

14. "Oh no, oh no, my brither dear,
 The clans they are ower strang,
An they drive back our merry men,
 Wi swords baith sharp an lang."

15. Brave Forbës drew his men aside,
 Said, Tak your rest a while,
Until I to Drumminnor send,
 To fess my coat o mail.

16. The servan he did ride,
 An his horse it did na fail,
For in twa hours an a quarter
 He brocht the coat o mail.

17. Then back to back the brithers twa
 Gaed in amo the thrang,
An they hewed doun the Hielanmen,
 Wi swords baith sharp and lang.

18. Macdonell, he was young an stout,
 Had on his coat o mail,
An he has gone oot throw them a',
 To try his han himsell.

19. The first ae straik that Forbës strack,
 He garrt Macdonell reel,
An the neist ae straik that Forbës strack,
 The great Macdonell fell.

20. An siccan a lierachie
 I'm sure ye never saw
As wis amo the Hielanmen,
 When they saw Macdonell fa.

21. An whan they saw that he was deid,
 They turnd an ran awa,

An they buried him in Leggett's Den,
   A large mile frae Harlaw.

22. They rade, they ran, an some did gang,
      They were o sma record;
    But Forbës an his merry men,
      They slew them a' the road,

23. On Monanday, at mornin,
      The battle it began,
    On Saturday, at gloamin,
      Ye'd scarce kent wha had wan.

24. An sic a weary buryin
      I'm sure ye never saw
    As wis the Sunday after that,
      On the muirs aneath Harlaw.

25. Gin ony body speer at you
      For them ye took awa,
    Ye may tell their wives and bairnies
      They're sleepin at Harlaw.

XLI

Johnie Armstrong

As pointed out in the Introduction (p. 43), *Ihonne Ermistrangis dance* is
one of the traditional songs mentioned in *The Complaynt of Scotland* (1549).
The Armstrongs appear to have been a clan of considerable power in
the Debateable Lands of the Border, with their main stronghold at Mangerton, in Liddesdale. From 1525 onward John Armstrong troubled both
the English and Scots by forays and cattle-raids, until he was brought to
heel, probably by treachery, in 1530 after an armed expedition under
King James V of Scotland.

1. There dwelt a man in faire Westmerland,
      Ionnë Armestrong men did him call,

He had nither lands nor rents coming in,
    Yet he kept eight score men in his hall.

2. He had horse and harness for them all,
    Goodly steeds were all milke-white;
O the golden bands an about their necks,
    And their weapons, they were all alike.

3. Newes then was brought unto the king
    That there was sicke a won as hee,
That livëd lyke a bold out-law,
    And robbëd all the north country.

4. The king he writt an a letter then,
    A letter which was large and long;
He signëd it with his owne hand,
    And he promised to doe him no wrong.

5. When this letter came Ionnë untill,
    His heart it was as blythe as birds on the tree:
"Never was I sent for before any king,
    My father, my grandfather, nor none but mee.

6. "And if wee goe the king before,
    I would we went most orderly;
Every man of you shall have his scarlet cloak,
    Laced with silver laces three.

7. "Every won of you shall have his velvett coat,
    Laced with sillver lace so white;
O the golden bands an about your necks,
    Black hatts, white feathers, all alyke."

8. By the morrow morninge at ten of the clock,
    Towards Edenburough gon was hee,
And with him all his eight score men;
    Good lord, it was a goodly sight for to see!

9. When Ionnë came befower the king,
     He fell downe on his knee;
   "O pardon, my soveraine leige," he said,
     "O pardon my eight score men and mee!"

10. "Thou shalt have no pardon, thou traytor strong,
     For thy eight score men nor thee;
   For to-morrow morning by ten of the clock,
     Both thou and them shall hang on the gallow-tree."

11. But Ionnë looke'd over his left shoulder,
     Good Lord, what a grevious look looked hee!
   Saying, Asking grace of a graceless face—
     Why there is none for you nor me.

12. But Ionnë had a bright sword by his side,
     And it was made of the mettle so free,
   That had not the king stept his foot aside,
     He had smitten his head from his faire boddë.

13. Saying, Fight on, my merry men all,
     And see that none of you be taine;
   For rather then men shall say we were hange'd,
     Let them report how we were slaine.

14. Then, God wott, faire Eddenburrough rose,
     And so besett poore Ionnë rounde,
   That fowerscore and tenn of Ionnës best men
     Lay gasping all upon the ground.

15. Then like a mad man Ionnë laide about,
     And like a mad man then fought hee,
   Untill a falce Scot came Ionnë behinde,
     And runn him through the faire boddee.

16. Saying, Fight on, my merry men all,
     And see that none of you be taine;

For I will stand by and bleed but awhile,
    And then will I come and fight againe.

17. Newes then was brought to young Ionnë Armestrong,
    As he stood by his nurses knee,
Who vowed if ere he live'd for to be a man,
    O the treacherous Scots revengd hee'd be.

XLII

Jock o the Side

John o the Side, another of the mid-sixteenth-century marauders of the Debateable Lands, can be traced in records between 1550 and 1569. He seems to have aided the Earl of Westmoreland after the failure of the Rising of the North.

1. Peeter a Whifeild he hath slaine,
    And Iohn a Side, he is tane,
And Iohn is bound both hand and foote,
    And to the New-castle he is gone.

2. But tydinges came to the Sybill o the Side,
    By the water-side as shee rann;
Shee tooke her kirtle by the hem,
    And fast shee runn to Mangerton.

3. .   .   .   .   .   .
    The lord was sett downe at his meate;
When these tydings shee did him tell,
    Neuer a morsell might he eate.

4. But lords, the wrunge their fingars white,
    Ladyes did pull themselues by the haire,
Crying, Alas and weladay!
    For Iohn o the Side wee shall neuer see more.

5. "But wee'le goe sell our droues of kine,
   And after them our oxen sell,
   And after them our troopes of sheepe,
   But wee will loose him out of the New Castell."

6. But then bespake him Hobby Noble,
   And spoke these words wonderous hye;
   Sayes, Giue me fiue men to my selfe,
   And I'le feitch Iohn o the Side to thee.

7. "Yea, thou'st haue fiue, Hobby Noble,
   Of the best that are in this countrye;
   I'le giue thee fiue thousand, Hobby Noble,
   That walke in Tyuidale trulye."

8. "Nay, I'le haue but fiue," saies Hobby Noble,
   "That shall walke away with mee;
   Wee will ryde like noe men of warr;
   But like poore badgers wee wilbe."

9. They stuffet vp all their baggs with straw,
   And their steeds barefoot must bee;
   "Come on, my bretheren," says Hobby Noble,
   "Come on your wayes, and goe with mee."

10. And when they came to Culerton ford,
    The water was vp, they cold it not goe;
    And then they were ware of a good old man,
    How his boy and hee were at the plowe.

11. "But stand you still," sayes Hobby Noble,
    "Stand you still heere at this shore,
    And I will ryde to yonder old man,
    And see w[h]ere the gate it lyes ore.

12. "But Christ you saue, father!" quoth hee,
    "Crist both you saue and see!

Where is the way ouer this fford?
For Christ's sake tell itt mee!"

13. "But I haue dwelled heere three score yeere,
Soe haue I done three score and three;
I neuer sawe man nor horsse goe ore,
Except itt were a horse of tree."

14. "But fare thou well, thou good old man!
The devill in hell I leave with thee,
Noe better comfort heere this night
Thow giues my bretheren heere and me."

15. But when he came to his brether againe,
And told this tydings full of woe,
And then they found a well good gate
They might ryde ore by two and two.

16. And when they were come ouer the fforde,
All safe gotten att the last,
"Thankes be to God!" sayes Hobby Nobble,
"The worst of our perill is past."

17. And then they came into Howbrame wood,
And there then they found a tree,
And cutt itt downe then by the roote;
The lenght was thirty ffoote and three.

18. And four of them did take the planke,
As light as it had beene a fflee,
And carryed itt to the New Castle,
Where as Iohn a Side did lye.

19. And some did climbe vp by the walls,
And some did climbe vp by the tree,
Vntill they came vpp to the top of the castle,
Where Iohn made his moane trulye.

20. He sayd, God be with thee, Sybill o the Side!
　　　My owne mother thou art, quoth hee;
　If thou knew this night I were here,
　　　A woe woman then woldest thou bee.

21. And fare you well, Lord Mangerton!
　　　And euer I say God be with thee!
　For if you knew this night I were heere,
　　　You wold sell your land for to loose mee.

22. And fare thou well, Much, Millers sonne!
　　　Much, Millars sonne, I say;
　Thou has beene better att merke midnight
　　　Then euer thou was att noone o the day.

23. And fare thou well, my good Lord Clough!
　　　Thou art thy ffathers sonne and heire;
　Thou neuer saw him in all thy liffe
　　　But with him durst thou breake a speare.

24. Wee are brothers childer nine or ten,
　　　And sisters children ten or eleven.
　We neuer came to the feild to fight,
　　　But the worst of us was counted a man.

25. But then bespake him Hoby Noble,
　　　And spake these words vnto him;
　Saies, Sleepest thou, wakest thou, Iohn o the Side,
　　　Or art thou this castle within?

26. "But who is there," quoth Iohn oth Side,
　　　"That knowes my name soe right and free?"
　"I am a bastard-brother of thine;
　　　This night I am comen for to loose thee."

27. "Now nay, now nay," quoth Iohn o the Side;
　　　"Itt ffeares me sore that will not bee;

Ffor a pecke of gold and silver," Iohn sayd,
  "In faith this night will not loose mee."

28. But then bespake him Hobby Noble,
      And till his brother thus sayd hee;
    Sayes, Four shall take this matter in hand,
      And two shall tent our geldings ffree.

29. Four did breake one dore without,
      Then Iohn brake fiue himsell;
    But when they came to the iron dore,
      It smote twelue vpon the bell.

30. "Itt ffeares me sore," sayd Much, the Miller,
      "That heere taken wee all shalbee;"
    "But goe away, bretheren," sayd Iohn a Side,
      "For euer alas! this will not bee."

31. "But ffye vpon thee!" sayd Hobby Noble;
      "Much, the Miller, fye vpon thee!
    It sore feares me," said Hobby Noble,
      "Man that thou wilt neuer bee."

32. But then he had Fflanders files two or three,
      And hee fyled downe that iron dore,
    And tooke Iohn out of the New Castle,
      And sayd, Looke thou neuer come heere more!

33. When he had him fforth of the New Castle,
      "Away with me, Iohn, thou shalt ryde:"
    But euer alas! itt cold not bee;
      For Iohn cold neither sitt nor stryde.

34. But then he had sheets two or three,
      And bound Iohns boults fast to his ffeete,
    And sett him on a well good steede,
      Himselfe on another by him seete.

35. Then Hobby Noble smiled and loug[h]e,
    And spoke these worde in mickle pryde:
Thou sitts soe finely on thy geldinge
    That, Iohn, thou rydes like a bryde.

36. And when they came thorrow Howbrame towne,
    Iohns horsse there stumbled at a stone;
"Out and alas!" cryed Much, the Miller,
    "Iohn, thou'le make vs all be tane."

37. "But fye vpon thee!" saies Hobby Noble,
    "Much, the Millar, fye on thee!
I know full well," sayes Hobby Noble,
    "Man that thou wilt neuer bee."

38. And when the came into Howbrame wood,
    He had Fflanders files two or three
To file Iohns bolts beside his ffeete,
    That hee might ryde more easilye.

39. Sayes, "Iohn, now leape ouer a steede!"
    And Iohn then hee lope ouer fiue:
"I know well," sayes Hobby Noble,
    "Iohn, thy ffellow is not aliue."

40. Then he brought him home to Mangerton;
    The lord then he was att his meate;
But when Iohn o the Side he there did see,
    For faine hee cold noe more eate.

41. He sayes, Blest be thou, Hobby Noble,
    That euer thou wast man borne!
Thou hast feitched vs home good Iohn oth Side,
    That was now cleane ffrom vs gone.

XLIII

Jamie Telfer in the Fair Dodhead

Nothing is known about the exact historical background of this ballad; even the location of the farm of the Fair Dodhead is unknown. The Captain of Bewcastle, a town in the heart of the reiver country, appears to have taken a leaf out of the reiver's book. The sympathies of the poet are clearly with the robbed man, not, as in the three preceding ballads, with the robber. The "bringing of the fray" (the call for help against robbery) falls on deaf ears in the case of the laird of Buccleugh, because Jamie Telfer has paid no protection money ("blackmail") to him. But, as Jamie Telfer's race for help continues, we seem to move with breathless speed through the rough countryside, past the isolated, well-defended keeps and farmhouses, until we participate in the sudden fierce fray, and the Captain of Bewcastle's own cattle are taken to atone for his robbery; for Jamie and his associates are no better or worse than the Captain. The two elegiac stanzas thirty-five and thirty-six, interrupting the epic movement of the rest of the poem, are typical of Scottish balladry.

1. It fell about the Martinmas,
  When steads were fed wi corn and hay,
 The Captain of Bewcastle said to his lads,
  We'll into Tiviotdale and seek a prey.

2. The first ae guide that they met with
  Was high up in Hardhaugh swire,
 The second guide that they met with
  Was laigh down in Borthick water.

3. "What tidings, what tidings, my bonny guide?"
  "Nae tidings, nae tidings I hae to thee;
 But if ye'll gae to the Fair Dodhead
  Mony a cow's calf I'll let ye see."

4. When they came to the Fair Dodhead,
  Right hastily they clam the peel,
 They loosd the nolt out, ane and a',
  And ranshakled the house right weel.

5. Now Jamie's heart it was right sair,
    The tear ay rowing in his eye;
He pled wi the Captain to hae his gear,
    Or else revengëd he would be.

6. Bat the Captain turnd himsel about,
    Said, Man, there's naething in thy house
But an auld sword without a scabbard,
    That scarcely now would fell a mouse.

7. The moon was up and the sun was down,
    'Twas the gryming of a new-fa'n snaw;
Jamie Telfer has run eight miles barefoot
    Between Dodhead and Branxholm Ha.

8. And when he came to Branxholm Ha
    He shouted loud and cry'd weel he,
Till up bespake then auld Buccleugh,
    "Whae's this that brings the fray to me?"

9. "It's I, Jamie Telfer i the Fair Dodhead,
    And a harried man I think I be;
There's naething left i the Fair Dodhead
    But only wife and children three."

10. "Gae seek your succour frae Martin Elliot,
    For succour ye's get nane frae me;
Gae seek your succour where ye paid blackmail,
    For, man, ye never paid money to me."

11. Jamie he's turnd him round about,
    And ay the tear blinded his eye:
"I'se never pay mail to Scott again,
    Nor the Fair Dodhead I'll ever see."

12. Now Jamie is up the water-gate,
    Een as fast as he can drie,

Till he came to the Coultart Cleugh,
    And there he shouted and cry'd weel he.

13. Then up bespake him auld Jock Grieve,
    "Whae's this that bring[s] the fray to me?"
  "It's I, Jamie Telfer i the Fair Dodhead,
    And a harried man I think I be.

14. "There's naething left i the Fair Dodhead
    But only wife and children three,
  And sax poor calves stand i the sta,
    A' routing loud for their minnie."

15. "Alack, wae's me!" co auld Jock Grieve,
    "Alack, alack, and wae is me!
  For ye was married t' the auld sister,
    And I t' the younges[t] o the three."

16. Then he's taen out a bonny black,
    It was weel fed wi corn and hay,
  And set Jamie Telfer on his back,
    To the Catlock hill to take the fray.

17. When he came to the Catlock hill,
    He shouted loud and cry'd weel he;
  "Whae's that, whae's that?" co Martin's Hab,
    "Whae's this that brings the fray to me?"

18. "It's I, Jamie Telfer i the Fair Dodhead,
    And a harried man I think I be;
  There's neathing left i the Fair Dodhead
    But only wife and children three."

19. "Alack, wae's me!" co Martin's Hab,
    "Alack, awae, my heart is sair!
  I never came bye the Fair Dodhead
    That ever I faund thy basket bare."

20. Then he's taen out a bonny black,
    It was weel fed wi corn and hay,
And set Jamie Telfer on his back
    To the Pricken haugh to take the fray.

21. When he came to the Pricken haugh,
    He shouted loud and cry'd weel he;
Up then bespake auld Martin Elliot,
    "Whae's this that brings the fray to me?"

22. "It's I, Jamie Telfer i the Fair Dodhead,
    And a harried man I think I be;
There's naething left i the Fair Dodhead
    But only wife and children three."

23. "Ever alack!" can Martin say,
    "And ay my heart is sair for thee!
But fy, gar ca on Simmy my son,
    And see that he come hastily.

24. "Fy, gar warn the water-side,
    Gar warn it soon and hastily;
Them that winna ride for Telfer's kye,
    Let them never look i the face o me.

25. "Gar warn the water, braid and wide,
    And warn the Currers i the shaw;
When ye come in at the Hermitage slack,
    Warn doughty Willie o Gorrenberry."

26. The gear was driven the Frostily up,
    From the Frostily into the plain;
When Simmie lookëd him afore,
    He saw the kye right fast driving.

27. "Whae drives the kye," then Simmy can say,
    "To make an outspeckle o me?"

"It's I, the Captain o Bewcastle, Simmy,
   I winna lain my name frae thee."

28. "O will ye let the gear gae back?
     Or will ye do ony thing for me?"
   "I winna let the gear gae back,
     Nor naething, Simmy, I'll do for the[e].

29. "But I'll drive Jamie Telfer's kye
     In spite o Jamie Telfer's teeth and thee;"
   "Then by my sooth," can Simmy say,
     "I'll ware my dame's calfskin on thee.

30. "Fa on them, lads!" can Simmy say,
     "Fy, fa on them cruelly!
   For or they win to the Ritter ford
     Mony toom saddle there shall be."

31. But Simmy was striken oer the head,
     And thro the napskape it is gane,
   And Moscrop made a dolefull rage,
     When Simmy on the ground lay slain.

32. "Fy, lay on them!" co Martin Elliot,
     "Fy, lay on them cruelly!
   For ere they win to the Kershop ford,
     Mony toom saddle there shall be."

33. John o Biggam he was slain,
     And John o Barlow, as I heard say,
   And fifteen o the Captain's men
     Lay bleeding on the ground that day.

34. The Captain was shot through the head,
     And also through the left ba-stane;
   Tho he had livd this hundred years,
     He'd neer been loed by woman again.

35. The word is gane unto his bride,
       Een in the bower where she lay,
    That her good lord was in's enemy's land
       Since into Tiviotdale he led the way.

36. "I loord a had a winding sheed
       And helpd to put it oer his head,
    Or he'd been taen in's enemy's lands,
       Since he oer Liddle his men did lead."

37. There was a man in our company,
       And his name was Willie Wudëspurs:
    "There is a house in the Stanegarside,
       If any man will ride with us."

38. When they came to the Stanegarside,
       They bangd wi trees and brake the door,
    They loosd the kye out, ane and a',
       And set them furth our lads before.

39. There was an auld wif ayont the fire,
       A wee bit o the Captain's kin:
    "Whae loo[s]es out the Captain's kye,
       And sae mony o the Captain's men wi[t]hin?"

40. "I, Willie Wudëspurs, let out the kye,
       I winna lain my name frae thee,
    And I'll loose out the Captain's kye
       In spite o the Captain's teeth and thee."

41. Now on they came to the Fair Dodhead,
       They were a welcome sight to see,
    And instead of his ain ten milk-kye
       Jamie Telfer's gotten thirty and three.

XLIV

Mary Hamilton

Compare Introduction (pp. 19, 52) for notes on this ballad, of which over thirty variants have been recorded. Perhaps we shall never know the historical background of this, one of our most deeply moving ballads. Fusion of various sources, as in the case of *Lady Isabel and the Elf-knight* (p. 37), seems likely.

1. Word's gane to the kitchen,
   And word's gane to the ha,
   That Marie Hamilton gangs wi bairn
   To the hichest Stewart of a'.

2. He's courted her in the kitchen,
   He's courted her in the ha,
   He's courted her in the laigh cellar,
   And that was warst of a'.

3. She's tyed it in her apron
   And she's thrown it in the sea;
   Says, Sink ye, swim ye, bonny wee babe!
   You'l neer get mair o me.

4. Down then cam the auld queen,
   Goud tassels tying her hair:
   "O Marie, where's the bonny wee babe
   That I heard greet sae sair?"

5. "There was never a babe intill my room,
   As little designs to be;
   It was but a touch o my sair side,
   Come oer my fair bodie."

6. "O Marie, put on your robes o black,
   Or else your robes o brown,

For ye maun gang wi me the night,
To see fair Edinbro town."

7. "I winna put on my robes o black,
Nor yet my robes o brown;
But I'll put on my robes o white,
To shine through Edinbro town."

8. When she gaed up the Cannogate,
She laughd loud laughters three;
But whan she cam down the Cannogate
The tear blinded her ee.

9. When she gaed up the Parliament stair,
The heel cam aff her shee;
And lang or she cam down again
She was condemnd to dee.

10. When she cam down the Cannogate,
The Cannogate sae free,
Many a ladie lookd oer her window,
Weeping for this ladie.

11. "Ye need nae weep for me," she says,
"Ye need nae weep for me;
For had I not slain mine own sweet babe,
This death I wadna dee.

12. "Bring me a bottle of wine," she says,
"The best that eer ye hae,
That I may drink to my weil-wishers,
And they may drink to me.

13. "Here's a health to the jolly sailors,
That sail upon the main;
Let them never let on to my father and mother
But what I'm coming hame.

14. "Here's a health to the jolly sailors,
        That sail upon the sea;
    Let them never let on to my father and mother
        That I cam here to dee.

15. "Oh little did my mother think,
        The day she cradled me,
    What lands I was to travel through,
        What death I was to dee.

16. "Oh little did my father think,
        The day he held up me,
    What lands I was to travel through,
        What death I was to dee.

17. "Last night I washd the queen's feet,
        And gently laid her down;
    And a' the thanks I've gotten the nicht
        To be hangd in Edinbro town!

18. "Last nicht there was four Maries,
        The nicht there'l be but three;
    There was Marie Seton, and Marie Beton,
        And Marie Carmichael, and me."

XLV

Edom o Gordon

This moving ballad, which reminds one of the heroism displayed by
Burnt Njal and other men and women of Icelandic Saga, is based on an
incident in the troubled history of Aberdeenshire in the years immediately
after Mary Stuart's flight from Scotland (1568). Adam, or Edom, o
Gordon, a Catholic partisan of the Queen, sent his captain, Thomas Ker,
or Car, on an expedition against the Protestant Forbes clan, during which
Ker burnt the stronghold of the Forbes with all its inmates in the absence
of Alexander Forbes (or Hamilton), the head of the clan. The oldest
version of the ballad appears to have been committed to paper soon after

the occurrence, and may not be free from partisanship. Stanzas nineteen to twenty-two are poignant in the extreme, and the whole ballad is full of tenderest emotion.

1. It befell at Martynmas,
        When wether waxed colde,
    Captaine Care said to his men,
        We must go take a holde.

        Syck, sike, and to-towe sike,
            And sike and like to die;
        The sikest nighte that euer I abode,
            God lord haue mercy on me!

2. "Haille, master, and wether you will,
        And wether ye like it best;"
    "To the castle of Crecrynbroghe,
        And there we will take our reste."

3. "I knowe wher is a gay castle,
        Is builded of lyme and stone;
    Within their is a gay ladie,
        Her lord is riden and gone."

4. The ladie she lend on her castle-walle,
        She loked vpp and downe;
    There was she ware of an host of men,
        Come riding to the towne.

5. "Se yow, my meri men all,
        And se yow what I see?
    Yonder I see an host of men,
        I muse who they bee."

6. She thought he had ben her wed lord,
        As he comd riding home;
    Then was it traitur Captaine Care,
        The lord of Ester-towne.

7. They wer no soner at supper sett,
    Then after said the grace,
Or Captaine Care and all his men
    Wer lighte aboute the place.

8. "Gyue ouer thi howsse, thou lady gay,
    And I will make the a bande;
To-nighte thou shall ly within my armes,
    To-morrowe thou shall ere my lande."

9. Then bespacke the eldest sonne,
    That was both whitt and redde:
O mother dere, geue ouer your howsse,
    Or elles we shalbe deade.

10. "I will not geue ouer my hous," she saithe,
    "Not for feare of my lyffe;
It shalbe talked throughout the land,
    The slaughter of a wyffe.

11. "Fetch me my pestilett,
    And charge me my gonne,
That I may shott at yonder bloddy butcher,
    The lord of Easter-towne."

12. Styfly vpon her wall she stode,
    And lett the pellettes flee;
But then she myst the blody bucher,
    And she slew other three.

13. "[I will] not geue ouer my hous," she saithe,
    "Netheir for lord nor lowne;
Nor yet for traitour Captaine Care,
    The lord of Easter-towne.

14. "I desire of Captine Care,
    And all his bloddye band,

That he would saue my eldest sonne,
　　The eare of all my lande."

15. "Lap him in a shete," he sayth,
　　　"And let him downe to me,
　　And I shall take him in my armes,
　　　His waran shall I be."

16. The captayne sayd unto him selfe:
　　　Wyth sped, before the rest,
　　He cut his tonge out of his head,
　　　His hart out of his brest.

17. He lapt them in a handkerchef,
　　　And knet it of knotes three,
　　And cast them ouer the castell-wall,
　　　At that gay ladye.

18. "Fye vpon the, Captayne Care,
　　　And all thy bloddy band!
　　For thou hast slayne my eldest sonne,
　　　The ayre of all my land."

19. Then bespake the yongest sonne,
　　　That sat on the nurses knee,
　　Sayth, Mother gay, geue ouer your house;
　　　It smoldereth me.

20. "I wold geue my gold," she saith,
　　　"And so I wolde my ffee,
　　For a blaste of the westryn wind,
　　　To dryue the smoke from thee.

21. "Fy vpon the, John Hamleton,
　　　That euer I paid the hyre!
　　For thou hast broken my castle-wall,
　　　And kyndled in the ffyre."

22. The lady gate to her close parler,
    The fire fell aboute her head:
    She toke vp her children thre,
    Seth, Babes, we are all dead.

23. Then bespake the hye steward,
    That is of hye degree;
    Saith, Ladie gay, you are in close,
    Wether ye fighte or flee.

24. Lord Hamleton dremd in his dream,
    In Caruall where he laye,
    His halle were all of fyre,
    His ladie slayne or daye.

25. "Busk and bowne, my mery men all,
    Even and go ye with me;
    For I dremd that my haal was on fyre,
    My lady slayne or day."

26. He buskt him and bownd hym,
    And like a worthi knighte;
    And when he saw his hall burning,
    His harte was no dele lighte.

27. He sett a trumpett till his mouth,
    He blew as it plesd his grace;
    Twenty score of Hamlentons
    Was light aboute the place.

28. "Had I knowne as much yesternighte
    As I do to-daye,
    Captaine Care and all his men
    Should not haue gone so quite.

29. "Fye vpon the, Captaine Care,
    And all thy blody bande!

Thou haste slayne my lady gay,
  More wurth then all thy lande.

30. "If thou had ought eny ill will," he saith,
   "Thou shoulde haue taken my lyffe,
And haue saved my children thre,
   All and my louesome wyffe."

XLVI

The Bonnie House of Airlie

Like *Edom o Gordon*, this ballad deals with the burning and pillaging
of a noble house, and a lady's courage in the face of oppression. The tone
of this ballad is less ferocious and more elegiac.

The actual event occurred in 1640, when the Earl of Argyle, in exces-
sively harsh pursuance of a royal commission, harried religious oppo-
nents with fire and sword.

1. It fell on a day, and a bonny summer day,
   When corn grew green and yellow,
That there fell out a great dispute
   Between Argyll and Airly.

2. Argyll has raisd an hundred men,
   An hundred men, and so many,
And he is away by the back of Dunkeld,
   For to plunder the bonny house of Airly.

3. Lady Margaret looks oer her bower-window,
   And O but she looks weary!
And there she spied the great Argyll,
   Coming to plunder the bonny house of Airly.

4. "Come down, come down, Lady Margret," he said,
   "Come down, and kiss me fairly:"

"O I will not kiss the great Argyll,
  If he should not leave a standing stone in Airly."

5. He hath taken her by the left shoulder,
     Says, Lady where lyes thy dowry?
   "It's up and it's down by the bonny bank-side,
     Amongst the planting of Airly."

6. They have sought it up, they have sought it down,
     They have sought it both late and early,
   And they have found it in the bonny plumb-tree
     That shines on the bowling-green of Airly.

7. He hath taken her by the middle so small,
     And O but she lookd weary!
   He hath laid her down by the bonny burn-side,
     Till he hath plundered the bonny house of Airly.

8. "If my good lord were at home this night,
     As he is with Prince Charly,
   Nouther you nor no Scottish lord
     Durst have set a foot on the bowling-green of
       Airly.

9. "Ten bonny sons I have born unto him,
     The eleventh neer saw his daddy;
   Although I had an hundred more,
     I would give them all to Prince Charly."

XLVII

The Fire of Frendraught

The fire in which two young Scottish lairds were killed while staying
at the house of the Frendraughts, whom they had assisted in allaying an
old feud, occurred in 1630. Whether or not the fire was an accident, the

ballad poet preferred to see in Lady Frendraught a Lady Macbeth, and in her two victims gallant youths bound to each other by the closest links of friendship. The differences between the extant variants may indicate the readiness of the ballad poet to recount events as they should have happened rather than as they did.

1. The eighteenth of October,
     A dismal tale to hear
   How good Lord John and Rothiemay
     Was both burnt in the fire.

2. When steeds was saddled and well bridled,
     And ready for to ride,
   Then out it came for false Frendraught,
     Inviting them to bide.

3. Said, "Stay this night untill we sup,
     The morn untill we dine;
   'T will be a token of good greement
     'Twixt your good lord and mine."

4. "We'll turn again," said good Lord John;
     "But no," said Rothiemay,
   "My steed's trapand, my bridle's broken,
     I fear the day I'm fey."

5. When mass was sung, and bells was rung,
     And all men bound for bed,
   Then good Lord John and Rothiemay
     In one chamber was laid.

6. They had not long cast off their cloaths,
     And were but now asleep,
   When the weary smoke began to rise,
     Likewise the scorching heat.

7. "O waken, waken, Rothiemay!
     O waken, brother dear!

And turn you to our Saviour;
  There is strong treason here."

8. When they were dressed in their cloaths,
    And ready for to boun,
  The doors and windows was all secur'd,
    The roof-tree burning down.

9. He did him to the wire-window,
    As fast as he could gang;
  Says, Wae to the hands put in the stancheons!
    For out we'll never win.

10. When he stood at the wire-window,
    Most doleful to be seen,
  He did espy her Lady Frendraught,
    Who stood upon the green.

11. Cried, Mercy, mercy, Lady Frendraught!
    Will ye not sink with sin?
  For first your husband killed my father,
    And now you burn his son.

12. O then out spoke her Lady Frendraught,
    And loudly did she cry;
  "It were great pity for good Lord John,
    But none for Rothiemay;
  But the keys are casten in the deep draw-well,
    Ye cannot get away."

13. While he stood in this dreadful plight,
    Most piteous to be seen,
  There called out his servant Gordon,
    As he had frantic been:

14. "O loup, O loup, my dear master!
    O loup and come to me!

I'll catch you in my arms two,
    One foot I will not flee.

15. "O loup, O loup, my dear master!
    O loup and come away!
I'll catch you in my arms two,
    But Rothiemay may lie."

16. "The fish shall never swim in the flood,
    Nor corn grow through the clay,
Nor the fiercest fire that ever was kindled
    Twin me and Rothiemay.

17. "But I cannot loup, I cannot come,
    I cannot win to thee;
My head's fast in the wire-window,
    My feet burning from me.

18. "My eyes are seething in my head,
    My flesh roasting also,
My bowels are boiling with my blood;
    Is not that a woeful woe?

19. "Take here the rings from my white fingers,
    That are so long and small,
And give them to my lady fair,
    Where she sits in her hall.

20. "So I cannot loup, I cannot come,
    I cannot loup to thee;
My earthly part is all consumed,
    My spirit but speaks to thee."

21. Wringing her hands, tearing her hair,
    His lady she was seen,
And thus addressed his servant Gordon,
    Where he stood on the green.

22. "O wae be to you, George Gordon!
        An ill death may you die!
    So safe and sound as you stand there,
        And my lord bereaved from me."

23. "I bad him loup, I bad him come,
        I bad him loup to me;
    I'd catch him in my arms two,
        A foot I should not flee.   &c.

24. "He threw me the rings from his white fingers,
        Which were so long and small,
    To give to you, his lady fair,
        Where you sat in your hall."   &c.

25. Sophia Hay, Sophia Hay,
        O bonny Sophia was her name,
    Her waiting maid put on her cloaths,
        But I wot she tore them off again.

26. And aft she cried, Ohon! alas! alas!
        A sair heart's ill to win;
    I wan a sair heart when I married him,
        And the day it's well returnd again.

XLVIII

The Bonny Earl of Murray

The following three ballads resemble each other in their elegiac note: gallant men, full of promise, cut off prematurely as the result of clan feud or political violence, are mourned by the poet or take leave of their dear ones and of their possessions. The short-line stanzas of this ballad and of one or two others seem to add a special poignancy, and to relate these ballads to the Gaelic coronachs, or dirges.

The Earl of Murray of this ballad was the son-in-law of the Regent

Murray, and was murdered by the Regent's enemy the Earl of Huntly-
in 1592, in the course of the disturbances under Bothwell.

1. Ye Highlands, and ye Lawlands,
   Oh where have you been?
   They have slain the Earl of Murray,
   And they layd him on the green.

2. "Now wae be to thee, Huntly!
   And wherefore did you sae?
   I bade you bring him wi you,
   But forbade you him to slay."

3. He was a braw gallant,
   And he rid at the ring;
   And the bonny Earl of Murray,
   Oh he might have been a king!

4. He was a braw gallant,
   And he playd at the ba;
   And the bonny Earl of Murray
   Was the flower amang them a'.

5. He was a braw gallant,
   And he playd at the glove;
   And the bonny Earl of Murray,
   Oh he was the Queen's love!

6. Oh lang will his lady
   Look oer the castle Down,
   Eer she see the Earl of Murray
   Come sounding thro the town!
   Eer she, etc.

XLIX

Willie Macintosh

It is interesting to note that, according to Child, this ballad, using history for legitimate poetical purposes of concentration, fuses two distinct characters: the burning of Auchindown by the first William Macintosh took place in 1500, while the encounter between the second Macintosh and the Earl of Huntly near the Stapliegate (a hill in the North Highlands) took place in 1592, and formed another violent episode in the civil wars under the Regent, Murray. The Macintoshes at that time wished to avenge the murder of the Bonny Earl of the last ballad, but were overwhelmed by Huntly.

1. "Turn, Willie Macintosh,
      Turn, I bid you;
   Gin ye burn Auchindown,
      Huntly will head you."

2. "Head me or hang me,
      That canna fley me;
   I'll burn Auchendown
      Ere the life lea me."

3. Coming down Deeside,
      In a clear morning,
   Auchindown was in flame,
      Ere the cock-crawing.

4. But coming oer Cairn Croom,
      And looking down, man,
   I saw Willie Macintosh
      Burn Auchindown, man.

5. "Bonny Willie Macintosh,
      Whare left ye your men?"
   "I left them in the Stapler,
      But they'll never come hame."

6. "Bonny Willie Macintosh,
       Whare now is your men?"
   "I left them in the Stapler,
       Sleeping in their sheen."

L

Bonnie James Campbell

The hero of this fine elegiac ballad has up to now escaped identification.

1. O it's up in the Highlands,
       and along the sweet Tay,
   Did bonie James Campbell
       ride monie a day.

2. Sadled and bridled,
       and bonie rode he;
   Hame came horse, hame came sadle,
       but neer hame cam he.

3. And doun cam his sweet sisters,
       greeting sae sair,
   And down cam his bonie wife,
       tearing her hair.

4. "My house is unbigged,
       my barn's unbeen,
   My corn's unshorn,
       my meadow grows green."

*   *   *   *   *

LI

Lord Maxwell's Last Goodnight

In 1608 Lord Maxwell killed Sir James Johnstone, an old adversary, and fled overseas, but was executed on his return four years later.

This noble elegiac poem gains immeasurably by the roll-call of places loved and remembered.

1. "Adiew, madam my mother dear,
    But and my sisters two!
   Adiew, fair Robert of Oarchyardtoan!
    For thee my heart is woe.

2. "Adiew, the lilly and the rose,
    The primrose, sweet to see!
   Adiew, my lady and only joy!
    For I manna stay with thee.

3. "Tho I have killed the laird Johnston,
    What care I for his feed?
   My noble mind dis still incline;
    He was my father's dead.

4. "Both night and day I laboured oft
    Of him revenged to be,
   And now I've got what I long sought;
    But I manna stay with thee.

5. "Adiew, Drumlanrig! false was ay,
    And Cloesburn! in a band,
   Where the laird of Lagg fra my father fled
    When the Johnston struck off his hand.

6. "They were three brethren in a band;
    Joy may they never see!

But now I've got what I long sought,
And I maunna stay with thee.

7. "Adiew, Dumfries, my proper place,
   But and Carlaverock fair,
   Adiew, the castle of the Thrieve,
   And all my buildings there!

8. "Adiew, Lochmaben's gates so fair,
   The Langholm shank, where birks they be!
   Adiew, my lady and only joy!
   And, trust me, I maunna stay with thee.

9. "Adiew, fair Eskdale, up and down,
   Where my poor friends do dwell!
   The bangisters will ding them down,
   And will them sore compel.

10. "But I'll revenge that feed mysell
    When I come ou'r the sea;
    Adiew, my lady, and only joy!
    For I maunna stay with thee."

11. "Lord of the land, will you go then
    Unto my father's place,
    And walk into their gardens green,
    And I will you embrace.

12. "Ten thousand times I'll kiss your face,
    And sport, and make you merry";
    "I thank thee, my lady, for thy kindness,
    But, trust me, I maunna stay with thee."

13. Then he took off a great gold ring,
    Where at hang signets three:
    "Hae, take thee that, my ain dear thing,
    And still hae mind of me.

14. "But if thow marry another lord
      Ere I come ou'r the sea—
    Adiew, my lady and only joy!
      For I maunna stay with thee."

15. The wind was fair, the ship was close,
      That good lord went away,
    And most part of his friends were there,
      To give him a fair convay.

16. They drank thair wine, they did not spare,
      Even in the good lord's sight;
    Now he is oer the floods so gray,
      And Lord Maxwell has taen his goodnight.

LII

Bonny Baby Livingston

This ballad and the following one are concerned with violent abductions of Lowland girls by Highland men, a common enough occurrence
in the Border area up to the eighteenth century. The historical background of this ballad is difficult to ascertain, and was probably only dimly
known to the poet. It is interesting to note that all the extant versions
of this ballad, except the one given here, end tragically, and it may well
be that the happy ending of this version was introduced by the poet for
the sake of the romantic effect.

1. O bonny Baby Livingston
     Went forth to view the hay,
   And by it came him Glenlion,
     Sta bonny Baby away.

2. O first he's taen her silken coat,
     And neest her satten gown,
   Syne rowd her in a tartan plaid,
     And hapd her round and rown.

3. He has set her upon his steed
     And roundly rode away,
   And neer loot her look back again
     The live-long summer's day.

4. He's carried her oer hills and muirs
     Till they came to a Highland glen,
   And there he's met his brother John,
     With twenty armed men.

5. O there were cows, and there were ewes,
     And lasses milking there,
   But Baby neer anse lookd about,
     Her heart was filld wi care.

6. Glenlion took her in his arms,
     And kissd her, cheek and chin;
   Says, I'd gie a' these cows and ewes
     But ae kind look to win.

7. "O ae kind look ye neer shall get,
     Nor win a smile frae me,
   Unless to me you'll favour shew,
     And take me to Dundee."

8. "Dundee, Baby? Dundee, Baby?
     Dundee you neer shall see
   Till I've carried you to Glenlion
     And have my bride made thee.

9. "We'll stay a while at Auchingour,
     And get sweet milk and cheese,
   And syne we'll gang to Glenlion,
     And there live at our ease."

10. "I winna stay at Auchingour,
     Nor eat sweet milk and cheese,

Nor go with thee to Glenlion,
   For there I'll neer find ease."

11. Than out it spake his brother John,
   "O were I in your place,
I'd take that lady hame again,
   For a' her bonny face.

12. "Commend me to the lass that's kind,
   Tho na so gently born;
And, gin her heart I coudna gain,
   To take her hand I'd scorn."

13. "O had your tongue now, John," he says,
   "You wis na what you say;
For I've lood that bonny face
   This twelve month and a day.

14. "And tho I've lood her lang and sair
   A smile I neer coud win;
Yet what I've got anse in my power
   To keep I think nae sin."

15. When they came to Glenlion castle,
   They lighted at the yate,
And out it came his sisters three,
   Wha did them kindly greet.

16. O they've taen Baby by the hands
   And led her oer the green,
And ilka lady spake a word,
   But bonny Baby spake nane.

17. Then out it spake her bonny Jean,
   The youngest o the three,
"O lady, dinna look sae sad,
   But tell your grief to me."

18. "O wherefore should I tell my grief,
Since lax I canna find?
I'm stown frae a' my kin and friends,
And my love I left behind.

19. "But had I paper, pen, and ink,
Before that it were day,
I yet might get a letter sent
In time to Johny Hay."

20. O she's got paper, pen, and ink,
And candle that she might see,
And she has written a broad letter
To Johny at Dundee.

21. And she has gotten a bonny boy,
That was baith swift and strang,
Wi philabeg and bonnet blue,
Her errand for to gang.

22. "O boy, gin ye'd my blessing win
And help me in my need,
Run wi this letter to my love,
And bid him come wi speed.

23. "And here's a chain of good red gowd,
And gowdn guineas three,
And when you've well your errand done,
You'll get them for your fee."

24. The boy he ran oer hill and dale,
Fast as a bird coud flee,
And eer the sun was twa hours height
The boy was at Dundee.

25. And when he came to Johny's door
He knocked loud and sair;

Then Johny to the window came,
　　And loudly cry'd, "Wha's there?"

26. "O here's a letter I have brought,
　　Which ye maun quickly read,
　　And, gin ye woud your lady save,
　　Gang back wi me wi speed."

27. O when he had the letter read,
　　An angry man was he;
　　He says, Glenlion, thou shalt rue
　　This deed of villany!

28. "O saddle to me the black, the black,
　　O saddle to me the brown,
　　O saddle to me the swiftest steed
　　That eer rade frae the town.

29. "And arm ye well, my merry men a',
　　And follow me to the glen,
　　For I vow I'll neither eat nor sleep
　　Till I get my love again."

30. He's mounted on a milk-white steed,
　　The boy upon a gray,
　　And they got to Glenlion's castle
　　About the close of day.

31. As Baby at her window stood,
　　The west wind saft did bla;
　　She heard her Johny's well-kent voice
　　Beneath the castle wa.

32. "O Baby, haste, the window jump!
　　I'll kep you in my arm;
　　My merry men a' are at the yate,
　　To rescue you frae harm."

33. She to the window fixt her sheets
        And slipped safely down,
     And Johny catchd her in his arms,
        Neer loot her touch the ground.

34. When mounted on her Johny's horse,
        Fou blithely did she say,
     "Glenlion, you hae lost your bride!
        She's aff wi Johny Hay."

35. Glenlion and his brother John
        Were birling in the ha,
     When they heard Johny's bridle ring,
        As first he rade awa.

36. "Rise, Jock, gang out and meet the priest,
        I hear his bridle ring;
     My Baby now shall be my wife
        Before the laverocks sing."

37. "O brother, this is not the priest;
        I fear he'll come oer late;
     For armed men with shining brands
        Stand at the castle-yate."

38. "Haste Donald, Duncan, Dugald, Hugh!
        Haste, take your sword and spier!
     We'll gar these traytors rue the hour
        That eer they ventured here."

39. The Highland men drew their claymores,
        And gae a warlike shout,
     But Johny's merry men kept the yate,
        Nae ane durst venture out.

40. The lovers rade the live-lang night,
        And safe gat on their way,

And bonny Baby Livingston
Has gotten Johny Hay.

41. "Awa, Glenlion! fy for shame!
    Gae hide ye in some den!
  You've lettn your bride be stown frae you,
    For a' your armed men."

LIII

Rob Roy

The 'hero' of this ballad was the youngest son of Sir Walter Scott's
Rob Roy. He abducted a young widow, forced her to marry him, but was
arrested and executed in 1754.

1. Rob Roy, frae the high Highlands,
    Came to the Lawlan border;
  It was to steel a lady away,
    To keep his Highland house in order.

2. As he came in by White House,
    He sent nae ane before him;
  Or she wad hae secured the house,
    For she did ay abhor him.

3. Twenty men surrount the house, an twenty
    they went in,
    They found her wi her mither;
  Wi sighs an cries an watery eyes
    They parted fra ane anither.

4. "O will ye be my dear?" he says,
    "Or will ye be my honnie?
  O will ye be my wedded wife?
    I lee you best of ony."

5. "I winna be your dear," [she says,]
    "Nor will I be your honnie,
Nor will I be your wedded wife;
    Ye lee me for my money."

6. .   .   .   . by the way,
    This lady aftimes fainted;
Says, Woe be to my cursed gold,
    This road for me's invented!

7. He gave her no time for to dress
    Like ladies when they're ridin,
But set her on hie horseback,
    Himsell was ay beside her.

8. Whan they came to the Black House,
    And at Stirling tarried,
There he bought her coat an gown,
    But she would not [be] married.

9. Four men held her to the priest,
    An four they did her bed,
Wi sighs an cries an watery eyes
    Whan she by him was laid.

10. "Be content, be content,
    Be content wi me, lady;
Now ye are my wedded wife
    Untill the day ye die, lady.

11. "My father was a Highlan laird,
    McGrigor was his name, lady;
A' the country roun about
    They dreadit his great fame, lady.

12. "He kept a hedge about his land,
    A prickle to his foes, lady,

An every ane that did him wrang,
    He took him by the nose, lady.

13. "My father he delights in nout and goats,
    An me in horse and sheep, lady;
You and twenty thousan pound
    Makes me a man complete, lady.

14. You're welcome to this Highlan lan,
    It is my native plain, lady;
Think nae mair of gauin back,
    But tak it for your hame, lady.

15. "I'm gauin, [I'm gauin,]
    I'm gauin to France, lady;
Whan I come back
    I'll learn ye a dance, lady.

16. "Set your foot, [set your foot,]
    Set your foot to mine, lady;
Think nae mair of gauin back,
    But tak it for your hame, lady."

HUMOROUS BALLADS

LIV

Our Goodman

There is much of Chaucer's indomitable gaiety in this ballad. The questions of the jealous husband and the evasions of his wife are treated here in a humorous vein, and there are French ballads of a similar type. But *Clerk Saunders* shows that the same technique was used by ballad poets for a tragic purpose, and one of the finest Spanish popular ballads on a similar subject achieves tragic grandeur, not unlike that of our *Edward*, by the same technique.

1. Hame came our goodman,
    And hame came he.
   And then he saw a saddle-horse,
    Where nae horse should be.

2. "What's this now, goodwife?
    What's this I see?
   How came this horse here,
    Without the leave o me?"

   Recitative. "A horse?" quo she.
   "Ay, a horse," quo he.

3. "Shame fa your cuckold face,
    Ill mat ye see!
   'T is naething but a broad sow,
    My minnie sent to me."

   "A broad sow?" quo he.
   "Ay, a sow," quo shee.

4. "Far hae I ridden,
    And farer hae I gane,

But a sadle on a sow's back
    I never saw nane."

5. Hame came our goodman,
    And hame came he;
He spy'd a pair of jack-boots,
    Where nae boots should be.

6. "What's this now, goodwife?
    What's this I see?
How came these boots here,
    Without the leave o me?"

    "Boots?" quo she.
    "Ay, boots," quo he.

7. "Shame fa your cuckold face,
    And ill mat ye see!
It's but a pair of water-stoups,
    My minnie sent to me."

    "Water-stoups?" quo he.
    "Ay, water-stoups," quo she.

8. "Far hae I ridden,
    And farer hae I gane,
But siller spurs on water-stoups
    I saw never nane."

9. Hame came our goodman,
    And hame came he,
And he saw a sword,
    Whare a sword should na be.

10. "What's this now, goodwife?
    What's this I see?

How came this sword here,
  Without the leave o me?"

"A sword?" quo she.
"Ay, a sword," quo he.

11. "Shame fa your cuckold face,
      Ill mat ye see!
    It's but a porridge-spurtle,
      My minnie sent to me."

"A spurtle?" quo he.
"Ay, a spurtle," quo she.

12. "Far hae I ridden,
      And farer hae I gane,
    But siller-handed spurtles
      I saw never nane."

13. Hame came our goodman,
      And hame came he;
    There he spy'd a powderd wig,
      Where nae wig shoud be.

14. "What's this now, goodwife?
      What's this I see?
    How came this wig here,
      Without the leave o me?"

"A wig?" quo she.
"Ay, a wig," quo he.

15. "Shame fa your cuckold face,
      And ill mat you see!
    'T is naething but a clocken-hen,
      My minnie sent to me."

"Clocken hen?" quo he.
"Ay, clocken hen," quo she.

16. "Far hae I ridden,
        And farer hae I gane,
    But powder on a clocken-hen
        I saw never nane."

17. Hame came our goodman,
        And hame came he,
    And there he saw a muckle coat,
        Where nae coat shoud be.

18. "What's this now, goodwife?
        What's this I see?
    How came this coat here,
        Without the leave o me?"

"A coat?" quo she.
"Ay, a coat," quo he.

19. "Shame fa your cuckold face,
        Ill mat ye see!
    It's but a pair o blankets,
        My minnie sent to me."

"Blankets?" quo he.
"Ay, blankets," quo she.

20. "Far hae I ridden,
        And farer hae I gane,
    But buttons upon blankets
        I saw never nane."

21. Ben went our goodman,
        And ben went he,
    And there he spy'd a sturdy man,
        Where nae man shoud be.

22. "What's this now, goodwife?
      What's this I see?
How came this man here,
      Without the leave o me?"

"A man?" quo she.
"Ay, a man," quo he.

23. "Poor blind body,
      And blinder mat ye be!
It's a new milking-maid,
      My mither sent to me."

"A maid?" quo he.
"Ay, a maid," quo she.

24. "Far hae I ridden,
      And farer hae I gane,
But lang-bearded maidens
      I saw never nane."

LV

Get up and bar the Door

The slight touch of eeriness supplied by the midnight arrival of the two guests adds, by contrast, to the gusto of a ballad which looks like the retelling of a medieval fabliau (*i.e.*, comic verse-tale), possibly of Oriental antecedents.

1. It fell about the Martinmas time,
      And a gay time it was then,
When our goodwife got puddings to make,
      And she's boild them in the pan.

2. The wind sae cauld blew south and north,
      And blew into the floor;

Quoth our goodman to our goodwife,
"Gae out and bar the door."

3. "My hand is in my hussyfskap,
    Goodman, as ye may see;
An it shoud nae be barrd this hundred year,
    It's no be barrd for me."

4. They made a paction tween them twa,
    They made it firm and sure,
That the first word whaeer shoud speak,
    Shoud rise and bar the door.

5. Then by there came two gentlemen,
    At twelve o clock at night,
And they could neither see house nor hall,
    Nor coal nor candle-light.

6. "Now whether is this a rich man's house,
    Or whether is it a poor?"
But neer a word wad ane o them speak,
    For barring of the door.

7. And first they ate the white puddings,
    And then they ate the black;
Tho muckle thought the goodwife to hersel,
    Yet neer a word she spake.

8. Then said the one unto the other,
    "Here, man, tak ye my knife;
Do ye tak aff the auld man's beard,
    And I'll kiss the goodwife."

9. "But there's nae water in the house,
    And what shall we do than?"
"What ails ye at the pudding-broo,
    That boils into the pan?"

10. O up then started our goodman,
    An angry man was he:
    "Will ye kiss my wife before my een,
    And scad me wi pudding-bree?"

11. Then up and started our goodwife,
    Gied three skips on the floor;
    "Goodman, you've spoken the foremost word,
    Get up and bar the door."

LVI

The Wife wrapt in Wether's Skin

A popular tale may have given rise to this ballad, which might be entitled *The Wife of Bath Reformed*. The gay refrain underlines its humorous aspect. An American version opens with the lovely stanza:

Sweet William he married a wife
    (Gentle Jenny cried rosemaree)
To be the sweet comfort of his life
    (As the dew flies over the mulberry tree).

The "dew" in the second line of the refrain may be a corruption of "dove," but the line is one of the loveliest in poetry.

1. She wadna bake, she wadna brew
    Hollin, green hollin
    For spoiling o her comely hue,
    Bend your bow, Robin.

2. She wadna wash, she wadna wring,
    For spoiling o her gay goud ring.

3. Robin he's gane to the fald
    And catched a weather by the spauld.

4. And he has killed his weather black
    And laid the skin upon her back.

5. "I darena pay you, for your kin,
    But I can pay my weather's skin.

6. "I darena pay my lady's back,
    But I can pay my weather black."

7. "O Robin, Robin, lat me be,
    And I'll a good wife be to thee.

8. "It's I will wash, and I will wring,
    And never mind my gay goud ring.

9. "It's I will bake, and I will brew,
    And never mind my comely hue.

10. "And gin ye thinkna that eneugh,
    I'se tak the goad and I'se ca the pleugh.

11. "Gin ye ca for mair whan that is doon,
    I'll sit i the neuk and I'll dight your shoon."

LVII

The Farmer's Curst Wife

The surprising thing about this ballad is that the idea of a harridan who is too much for the devil can be traced back right across Europe to very early Indian saga.

1. There was an old farmer in Sussex did dwell,
        [*Chorus of whistlers*]
    There was an old farmer in Sussex did dwell,
    And he had a bad wife, as many knew well.
        [*Chorus of whistlers*]

2. Then Satan came to the old man at the plough:
    "One of your family I must have now.

3. "It is not your eldest son that I crave,
   But it is your old wife, and she I will have."

4. "O welcome, good Satan, with all my heart!
   I hope you and she will never more part."

5. Now Satan has got the old wife on his back,
   And he lugged her along, like a pedlar's pack.

6. He trudged away till they came to his hall-gate;
   Says he, Here, take in an old Sussex chap's mate.

7. O then she did kick the young imps about;
   Says one to the other, Let's try turn her out.

8. She spied thirteen imps all dancing in chains,
   She up with her pattens and beat out their brains.

9. She knocked the old Satan against the wall:
   "Let's turn her out, or she'll murder us all."

10. Now he's bundled her up on his back amain,
    And to her old husband he took her again.

11. "I have been a tormentor the whole of my life,
    But I neer was tormented so as with your wife."

GLOSSARY

This glossary contains only Scots or medieval English words the meaning of which is not evident from their context. The following rules will assist the reader in identifying Scots forms of common words:

1. English ō = Scots ā (written a, ae, or ai)
   (go = ga, gae; fro = fra; so = sae; sore = sair; stone = stane; rode = rade; oak = aik).
2. English oo = Scots ui or u
   (good = guid; blood = bluid; moor = muir).
3. English final -ll often disappears in Scots
   (all = a; hall = ha; pull = pu).
4. English final -g or -d is often dropped in Scots, especially after n- or l-
   (morning = mornin; hand = han; land = lan).

Words beginning with þ will be found under t(h), and those beginning with ȝ will be found under y.

a, a', all
abeen, aboon, above
abowght, about
ae, ever, one
aik, oak
airn, iron
aith, oath
alane, alone
ance, once
ane, if, one
ane, ain, own
archboard, stern of ship
aste, east
ayont, over against

ba, ball
badger, pedlar
baith, both
ban (1), curse
ban (2), band, hem

ban (3), bound
bande, bond, compact
bangisters, violent people
basnit, bassonet, light helmet
ba-stane, testicle
behad, behold
ben, within, inside
benbow, bent bow
bent, field (of battle)
berne, barn, warrior
bigget, built
bigley, commodious, habitable
billie, bullie, brother, comrade
birl, ply with drink
bit, but
bla, blow
blane, stopped
blin, stop
block, exchange
bomen, archers

boon, boun, bowyn, ready, make ready, go
boys, bows
boyt, both
bra, braw, fine, handsome
brae, hillside
braid, broad
braid letter, long letter
brain, mad
bree, brie, brow
breyde, rushed
brither, brother
bryttlynge, cutting up
busk, make ready, prepare
buss, bush
byckarte, attacked

ca, call
can, began
care-bed, sick-bed
carline, wealthy peasant woman
carnal, crow
cawte, wary
chamer, chamber
channer, fret
chiel, youth, boy
claith, clothing
clam, climbed
cleading, clothing
cleffe, cleave
clifting, fissure
clock, one who limps or hobbles
clocken hen, sitting hen
collayne, collen, of Cologne steel (*cp.* **myllan**)
coost, cast
corbie, raven
cors, curse
corsiare, courser
cressawntes, crescents
crowne, head

cumand, coming
curtes, courteous

dag-durk, dagger
dang (p. t. of **ding**), struck
dee (1), do
dee (2), die
deil, devil
dere, injury
dight, dressed
ding, beat, knock
dochter, daughter
dole, döl, dule, sorrow
doo, dow, dove
dorn, sheets of (Tournai) linen
dou, dought, be able, was able
dowie, sad
doyt, do
drap, drip
dree, drie, endure, undergo, be able
durre, door
dwell, hesitate

ee, een, eye, eyes
eie, awe
eme, uncle
eneugh, enough
envye, spite
ere, (verb) till
esk, newt
even (of cloth), smooth, like velvet

fa, fall
faem, foam
fail, turf
faine, joy
fairley, farly, thing of faery
fan, when
far, where

fash, turmoil
fat fadge, clumsy woman
feed, feud
feiries, comrades
fence, bout, coup
fess, fetch
ffooder, tun
firlot, measure of wine
fleed, stream, flood
fley, frighten
forfaulted, forfeited
fountain stane, font
fourfoughten, tired with fighting
freke, warrior
fringed, grey (of mane and fetlocks of horse)
frith, enclosed land
fu, full
fun, furze

ga, gae, go
gabber, sprightly
gaeng, gang, go
gallaly, galley
gar (*cp.* also **gars, gard, gartt**), cause
gare, piece of cloth
garl, gravel
gate, road
gaud, bar
ged, went
gi, gie (*cp.* also **gied, gin**), give
gimp, slender
gin (1), begin
gin (2), if
glent, glided
god, good
golett, throat-piece
gorget, neckerchief
goud, gold

gowan, daisy
graith, prepare
greement, agreement
greet, cry
grevis, groves
grimly, grumly, fierce
grith, peace
gryming, sprinkling
grype, gryphon
grysely, fearfully
gryte, great
guid, good
gyde (be), take charge of

ha, hall
hacheboard, gunwale, stern
hached, adorned
had, hold
hae, have
haik, keep in suspense
hale, whole
hall, hull, hold
hallow-seat, saint's place
halyde, hauled, pulled (of a bow)
hap (*cp.* **happit**), cover
haugh, low ground
hause-bane, collar-bone
he, high
heght, promised
height, be called
het, hot
hie, hurry
hind, hende, youth, young, courteous
hing, hang
holm, houm, low ground
hooly, slowly
houp, hollow between hills
houzle, Communion
hoved, tarried

huggle, hug, huddle

ilka, each, every

jobbing, billing (of doves)
jow, stroke (of bell)

kaivle, lot
kaim (verb and noun), comb
ken, know
kettrin, cateran, Highland
  marauder
kirkwa, church-wall
kirtle, woman's gown or skirt
knet, knotted
know, knoll, hill
ky, kine, cows

laigh, low
laily, loathly
lain(e), conceal, hide
lair, lore
lake, pit, cavity
lan, land
lap, jumped
lavrock, lark
lax, relief
lazar, leper
lea, lee, lie
lee, love
let, prevent
leugh, laughed
leven, lawn, forest glade
licht, alight, light
lierachie, hubbub
lig, lie
limmer, wretch
lin, stop
ling, rush, furse
Linkem, an indefinite ballad
  locality

lodly, loathsome
loe, lood, love, loved
lome, lame man
(hit is) long (of the), it is your
  responsibility
loot, let
loup, leap, jump
lour, loord, prefer
lout, bend, incline
lucettes, pikes
luppen (p.t. of **loup**), jumped

ma, mae, more
magger (in the), in spite of
mail (blackmail), protection-
  money
mane, complaint, moan
March-parti, Border region
mark, commend
marrow, mate
mary, lady's companion
mat, must
maun, must
maunna, must not
maut, malt
may, maiden
meal-pock, beggar's scrip
meany, maney, army, household
meen, moon
meikle, mickle, much
mell, mallet
minnie, mother
mither, mother
Moll Syms, sixteenth-century
  dance
moody-hill, mole-hill
mort, hunting-call, indicating
  death of deer
muir, moor
myllan, steel from Milan (*cp.*
  collayne)

myneyeple, manople, armour for hand and arm

napskape, headpiece
neest, neist, next
neuk, nook
nie, near
nolt, nout, neat, cattle
no noder, no other
nouther, neither
noy, grief

onfowghten, without fighting
ousen, oxen
outspeckle, laughing-stock
oware, hour
owtlay, outlaw

paction, agreement
pawage, road-tax
pay, give a beating
peel, tower, stronghold
pellettes, bullets
penny fee, alms of a penny
perte, part
pestilett, pistolet
philabeg, kilt
pick, pitch
pin, door-fastening, gallows-beam
piner-pig, earthen vessel for keeping money
pitten (p.p. of **pit**), put
plate-jack, plated upper garment
pleugh, plough
portmantua, satchel
prick, a mark in shooting
puggish, like a tramp, rugged
pyght, pitched
quo, quoth, said

quyrry, quarry

rad, afraid
rade, rede, rode
radly, quickly
ray, array, prepare
raysse, raid, warlike expedition
reas, raise, stir up
record (sma), of little note
rede, read, advise
reekit, smoky
reet, root
reiver, cattle-thief, especially on Scottish border
rig, ridge
rin, run
rock, distaff
roke, reek, vapour
roo, roe
rout, bellow
row (verb), wind
rowght, company
rowynde, round
rule, noisy wailing
rung, staff
ryall, royal
rynde and rent, flayed

sa, sae, so
sair, sore
sark, shirt, shift
satten, satin
saut, salt
sawten, assault
scad, scald
scaur, precipice, cliff
schoote, send away (of horse)
scroggs, brushwood
se, shall
seely court, fairy court
seld, sold

semblyde, assembled
sen, sent
settle by, set aside
shank, point of hill
shaw, wood
shed by, parted
sheen, bright, fair
sheene, sheyne, shoes
shouir, pang
sic, such
sichin, sichend, sighing
sicken-like, suchlike
simmer, summer
sin, sun
skinkled, sparkled
slack, low ground, pass
slon, slay
slough-hounds, sleuth-hounds
snell, sharp, brisk
somer, summer
Soudron, southern lands
sowens, flummery
sparred, bolted
spauld, shoulder
speer, spier, ask, inquire
spin, spurt
spole, shoulder
sprente, spurted
spulyie, take spoils, rob
spurn, contest
spurtle, stick for stirring por-
    ridge
sta, stolen
stage, stag
stane, stone
stank, ditch
stean, stone-seat
stour, stowre, battle
stown, stolen
straik (with a wand), even at
    the top by means of a stick

stratlins, stridings
straught, straight
streen (yestreen), yesternight
strete and stalle ⎫
strete and stye ⎬ everywhere
styrande, dislodging
suar, sure, trusty
sud, should
swarued, climbed
sweaven, sweven, dream
syke, ditch
syne, then, since

ta, tee (1), to
ta (2), take
tae, toe
taen, tain, tane, taken
taul, told
tent, heed
tett, lock
the (1), they
the (2), thrive
theek, thatch
thraw (cp. threw), twist, twine
thresel-cock, thrush
thurwardi, thorough
tiend, tithe
tirl, rattle at door-fastening
tift, puff
toom, empty
to-towe, all too
trapand, treacherously dealt with
    (of horse)
twal, twelve

unbeen, not thoroughly closed
unbigged, unbuilt
unco, strange
upgive, avow

vew-bow, bow of yew

wa, wae, woe

wad (noun), pledge

wad (verb), would

wael, choice

wall, well

wall-wight, well-wight, hand-picked

wallwood, wildwood

wane, crowd

wantonly, gaily

waran, warrant

wardl, world

warsle, struggle

waryson, reward

wast, west

wat, knew

water-gate, way along water

wed, pledge, forfeit

well-fared, handsome

wen (cp. weynde), wend, go

whidderand, whirring

wide, wade

widifus, one destined for the gallows

wight, bold

win, go, make one's way

wis, wist, know, knew

wite (verb and noun), blame

won, one

wood, mad

wood-wroth, furious

wouche, evil, harm

yae, one

yare, ready

yebent, bent

yefell, evil

yenoughe, enough

ye'se, yees, you shall

yete, got

yett, gate

yth, in the

SELECT BIBLIOGRAPHY

Collections of British Ballads

PERCY, BISHOP T.: *Reliques of Ancient English Poetry* (London, 1765).

SCOTT, SIR W.: *The Minstrelsy of the Scottish Border* (1802).

CHILD, F. J.: *English and Scottish Popular Ballads* (Boston; 5 vols., 1882–98).

ed. SARGENT, H. C., and KITTREDGE, G. L., *English and Scottish Popular Ballads* (Cambridge, Mass., 1904).

SHARP, C. J., and MARSON, C. L.: *Folk Songs from Somerset* (London, 1904–9).

SHARP, C. J.: *Songs and Ballads of the West* (London, 1905).

Folk Songs of England (London, 1908–11).

WILLIAMS, A.: *Folk Songs of the Upper Thames* (London, 1923).

Journal of the Folk Song Society (J.F.S.S.) (1899 onward) contains many fine ballad versions and ballad tunes, and is indispensable for a study of ballad music.

Collections of North American Ballads

McGILL, J.: *Folk Songs of the Kentucky Mountains* (1917).
CAMPBELL, O. D., and SHARP, C. J.: *English Folk Songs from the Southern Appalachians* (London, 1918).

English Translations of Foreign Ballads

RODD, T: *Spanish Ballads* (London, 1812).
GARNETT, L. M. J.: *Greek Folk Songs from the Turkish Provinces of Greece* (London, 1885).
GIBSON, J. Y.: *The Cid Ballads and other Poems* (London, 1898).
SMITH-DAMPIER, E. M.: *Danish Ballads* (Cambridge, 1920).
ROOTHAM, H.: *Kossovo* (*Heroic Songs of the Serbs*) (Oxford, 1920).
SUBOTIĆ, D.: *Yugoslav Popular Ballads* (Cambridge, 1932).
OLRIK, A., and SMITH-DAMPIER, E. M.: *A Book of Danish Ballads* (Oxford, 1939).

Critical Works

MARTINENGO-CESARESCO, E.: *Essays in the Study of Folk Songs* (London, 1886).
SHARP, C. J.: *English Folk Songs: Some Conclusions* (London, 1907).
GUMMERE, F. B.: *The Popular Ballad* (London, 1907).
POUND, L.: *Poetic Origins and the Ballad* (London, 1921).
KER, W. P.: "Spanish and English Ballads" and "On the Danish Ballads," I and II, *Collected Essays*, Vol. II (London, 1925).
Form and Style in Poetry (pp. 1–44) (London, 1928).
GEROULD, G. H.: *The Ballad of Tradition* (Oxford, 1932).
ENTWISTLE, W. J.: *European Balladry* (Oxford, 1939).
CHAMBERS, E. K.: *English Literature at the Close of the Middle Ages* (pp. 122–184) (Oxford, 1945).
HODGART, M. J. C.: *The Ballads* (London, 1950).